ESSENTIALS FOR STRATEGY & LEADERSHIP

> "Illuminate Your Path to Success with Strategic Guidance."
>
> —PREEA V MANE

ESSENTIALS FOR
STRATEGY &
LEADERSHIP
VISION TO VICTORY

Authored By,

Preea V Mane

<u>Disclaimer</u>

This book has been published with all reasonable efforts taken to make the material error-free after the consent of the author. This book is sold subject to the condition that it shall not, by way of trade or otherwise, be lent, resold, or otherwise circulated without the copyright owner's prior written consent in any form of binding or cover other than that in which it is published and without a similar condition including this condition being imposed on the subsequent purchaser and without limiting the rights under copyright reserved above, no part of this publication maybe reproduced, stored in or introduced into a retrieval system or transmitted in any form or by any other means without the permission of the copyright owner.

Registered Office- 907-Sneh Nagar, Sapna Sangeeta Road, Agrasen Square, Indore – 452001 (M.P.), India

Website: http://www.wingspublication.com

Email: mybook@wingspublication.com

First Published by WINGS PUBLICATION 2024

Copyright © Preea V Mane

Title : Essentials for Strategy & Leadership

Price : Rs. 999 I $ 25 I AED 85

All Rights Reserved.

ISBN : 978-93-6006-287-3

LIMITS OF LIABILITY/DISCLAIMER OF WARRANTY

About Author

Preea is a seasoned business executive with over 23 years of experience across diverse industries in senior leadership positions. With a specialization in commercial real estate, particularly within the Free Zone, she has spent more than 18 years honing her expertise in sales, marketing, and strategic planning. Her role as Vice President of Commercial involved overseeing the strategic direction and execution of all commercial real estate activities within her organization, driving revenue growth, forging strategic partnerships, and maximizing profitability by identifying emerging market trends and capitalizing on new business opportunities.

Preea has been awarded at the prestigious 2024 Excellence Awards by Gulf News and Being She at the prestigious event that seeks to honor the extraordinary women who have demonstrated exceptional leadership, innovation, and resilience in their respective fields. The annual awards ceremony is not just about celebrating success, it is about igniting a new era of recognition for exceptional women in the UAE and beyond.

Preea's strong background in sales and marketing has enabled her to develop and execute comprehensive strategies that enhance brand visibility, penetrate new markets, and achieve sustainable business growth. Her ability to combine data-driven insights with innovative ideas has led to the creation of highly effective go-to-market strategies. Throughout her career, she has played a pivotal role in driving revenue growth and maximizing profitability, leveraging her keen understanding of market dynamics and consumer behavior to develop targeted marketing campaigns and implement effective sales strategies.

Born in the sacred city of Nashik, Preea hails from a humble Kashmiri family that has inspired her to strive for excellence. Raised by a strong single mother alongside her siblings, she learned resilience and determination from a young age. Her upbringing was infused with values of compassion, integrity, and community, which have shaped her professional and personal ethos. Married into a Maharashtrian family with a diverse spectrum of accomplished individuals, Preea draws inspiration and strength from their unwavering support.

Education has always been paramount for Preea, a value deeply ingrained by her family. She holds a Bachelor of Commerce degree specializing in Entrepreneurship and Economics from Pune University, India, and a Master of Science in Leadership, Strategy, and Management from Michigan State University, USA. Her multifaceted journey spans interests in Entrepreneurship, Economics, Fashion Design, Multimedia, and Software

Engineering, beginning with ventures in Banking and Quality Management and extending to diverse sectors such as Design, Media, Technology, Innovation, and Sustainability.

Throughout her career, Preea has engaged with esteemed leaders and talented individuals across various industries, enriching her understanding of commercial real estate and broadening her expertise. Her immersive experiences have provided unique perspectives and challenges, fostering a holistic understanding of the broader economic landscape.

Preea is now dedicated to sharing her wealth of knowledge and experiences with aspiring entrepreneurs and talents, empowering them to chart their own paths to success. Beyond her professional pursuits, she is driven by a desire to give back to society, particularly the youth, and aims to inspire and empower the next generation of leaders through topics ranging from leadership and sustainability to technology and media.

Preea's journey is a testament to the power of resilience, determination, and unwavering ambition. As she continues to navigate the ever-evolving landscape of business and leadership, she remains committed to driving positive change, fostering innovation, and leaving a legacy for generations to come. Join her on this exciting journey of growth, exploration, and transformation.

Gratitude

I am deeply grateful to everyone who supported me throughout the creation of this book.

First and foremost, I want to express my deepest gratitude to God for guiding me through every step of my journey and blessing me with countless opportunities for growth and success.

To my beloved husband, Vickram, your unwavering support, love, and encouragement have been my rock. I am forever grateful for your presence in my life.

To my sons, Vishhal and Viivaan, you both bring immense joy and purpose to our family. Your laughter and love fill our home with warmth and happiness.

To my entire family, your love and support have been a constant source of strength and inspiration. I am blessed to have each of you in my life. Your belief in me has been a constant source of strength.

I extend my heartfelt appreciation to my friends and colleagues, whose insightful feedback and thoughtful discussions have significantly enriched this work.

Special thanks to my mentors and coaches, and a heartfelt appreciation to my editor and publisher, Dr. Kailash Pinjani and Dr. Deepak Parbat, for their professional guidance, dedication, and unwavering support in bringing this project to life.

Lastly, I am thankful to my readers for their interest and support. Your enthusiasm fuels my passion for writing.

With heartfelt gratitude, Preea

Dedication

This book is dedicated to all those who embody the essence of leadership, management, and strategic thinking. It pays tribute to those who dream big, navigate business complexities with grace, and inspire others through their actions and words.

To the visionaries who chart paths to success and drive progress through strategy and innovation, this book is for you.

To the managers who lead with empathy, integrity, and courage, empowering teams and fostering growth, this book is for you.

To the strategists who anticipate change, find opportunities in chaos, and shape the future of industries, this book is for you.

To all who pursue excellence and make positive impacts in their teams, organizations, and communities, this book is for you.

May the insights within these pages inspire and guide you on your journey toward achieving your goals. Your pursuit of excellence enriches the world around you.

With deepest gratitude and admiration,

Preea

Summary

This book underscores the significance of strategy, leadership, and management in achieving success within organizations. It emphasizes the value of having a clear vision, effective strategies, and proper execution. Key aspects such as goal understanding, creating unique value propositions, and prioritizing customer experience are highlighted.

Furthermore, the book explores various elements of strategy and its implementation, including resource optimization, risk management, and operations management. It also differentiates between leadership and management, with leadership focusing on inspiring and guiding teams, while management concentrates on delivering and implementing the vision.

The text discusses different management styles, such as visionary, coaching, autocratic, transformational, transactional, democratic, conflict resolution, and laissez-faire management, and their respective implications. Additionally, it delves into inclusive management, promoting equity, diversity, and inclusion, and advocates for creating an environment that fosters employee empowerment, trust, and collaboration.

Moreover, the book emphasizes key strategies for empowering employees, such as building a culture of trust, involving them in decision-making, providing growth opportunities, and recognizing their contributions. Overall, it highlights the importance of empowerment strategies in cultivating a positive work culture and driving organizational productivity. After reading this book, you'll walk away with a deeper understanding of how effective leadership, strategic thinking, and inclusive management can shape your professional roadmap and contribute to organizational success.

Contents

Preface

In the ever-evolving landscape of business and management, the convergence of strategy, leadership, and management emerges as a cornerstone for organisational success. As I embark on this journey of exploration and discovery, I am compelled to reflect on the profound interplay between these critical dimensions and their transformative impact on individuals, teams, and entire organisations.

This book is born out of a deep-seated passion for unravelling the intricacies of effective leadership, strategic thinking, and sound management practices. Through years of study, observation, and hands-on experience, I have come to appreciate the symbiotic relationship between strategy, leadership, and management – a relationship that transcends the boundaries of industry, geography, and organisational size.

At its core, this book seeks to demystify the art and science of navigating the complex terrain of modern business. From crafting visionary strategies to inspiring teams, from fostering a culture of innovation to driving operational excellence, each section is imbued with practical insights, real-world examples, and actionable strategies.

As I delve into the realms of strategy, leadership, and management, I invite you, the reader, to join me on a journey of exploration and growth. Together, we will traverse the peaks and valleys of organisational dynamics, uncovering hidden truths, dispelling myths, and charting a course towards sustainable success.

Whether you are a seasoned executive, an aspiring leader, or a curious enthusiast, this book is intended to serve as a guiding light on your quest for excellence. May it inspire you to embrace new perspectives, challenge conventional wisdom, and embark on a transformative journey of personal and professional growth.

As we embark on this voyage together, let us seize the opportunity to unlock our full potential, cultivate resilience in the face of adversity, and shape a future where strategic thinking, inspirational leadership, and effective management practices reign supreme.

Welcome to the nexus of Strategy, Leadership, and Management – where vision meets action, and possibilities abound.

Preea V Mane

Foreword

In an era where the pace of change is relentless and the demands on leaders are greater than ever, Preea's book 'Essentials for Strategy & Leadership – Vision to Victory' arrives as a beacon of insight. This book is not just a manual for those in leadership positions; it is a call to action for anyone who aspires to make a lasting impact within their organization.

Having had the privilege of observing Preea's career, I can attest to the depth of knowledge and experience she brings to the table. With a career spanning over two decades, she has navigated the complexities of diverse industries, from banking and media to technology and commercial real estate. Her expertise, particularly in the dynamic environment of Free Zones, has positioned her as a thought leader who understands the intricacies of strategic planning and effective leadership.

Moreover, Preea's emphasis on inclusive management practices is both timely and necessary. In a world that increasingly values diversity, equity, and inclusion, her advocacy for these principles as cornerstones of effective leadership is highly relevant. By fostering environments of trust and collaboration, leaders can unlock the full potential of their teams and drive sustained organizational success.

As you delve into this book, you will find not just strategies and tips, but a philosophy of leadership that is rooted in integrity, resilience, and a commitment to continuous growth. The author's insights are drawn from her own experiences—the challenges and the triumphs—and she shares them with great generosity.

Whether you are an emerging leader or a seasoned executive, this book will serve as a valuable resource on your journey. I invite you to embark on this transformative journey through the pages of this remarkable book.

Dr. Kailash Pinjani

Best Selling Author of ***"Date Your Clients"*** and
"Catch The Shark"

Testimonials

Preea's book 'Strategy & Leadership' is a must-read for anyone seeking to understand the critical role these elements play in driving organizational success. With her extensive experience across multiple industries and a deep understanding of leadership dynamics, Preea offers readers a comprehensive guide that bridges the gap between theory and practice. Her knowledge shines through every chapter

Dr Deepak Parbat

Best Selling Author of ***"Well Done You Are Hired"*** and

"A Monk In Suit"

Preea's insights into aligning objectives, creating unique value propositions, and prioritizing customer experience are invaluable for leaders at any stage of their careers. The book 'Strategy & Leadership' masterfully highlights the importance of a clear vision, effective strategies, and meticulous execution in achieving goals. It provides a nuanced understanding of different management styles and their impact on professional dynamics.

Ms Manika Singh
Best Selling Author of ***"Decoding Fitness"*** and
"Chakra Entrepreneur"

'Strategy & Leadership' is more than just a guide to leadership and strategy—it's a roadmap for empowering teams, fostering collaboration, and driving sustained organizational productivity. Preea's ability to distil complex concepts into actionable strategies makes this an indispensable resource for both aspiring and seasoned leaders. Her authority on these subjects is unquestionable.

Ms Simran Gangwani

Best Selling Author of **"7 Amazing Happiness Mantras"**

Introduction

STRATEGY, LEADERSHIP AND MANAGEMENT

Do you perceive these as mere three words? Within them lies a potent declaration, crucial for the success of any organisation, regardless of its industry, product, or service. The statement I discern is the creation of a successful brand through a simple strategy under the guidance of appropriate leadership and management.

Let's uncover the influence of these keywords and statements as we dive into the steps to attain the ultimate objective.

Remember, the mind, body, and soul are intertwined. It's essential to keep the mind grounded and aware. As you take a leap of faith, remain mindful and realistic.

Identifying Ultimate Goal

Declutter your mind!

Now is the moment to visualise your objective. Bring forth the vision! Trust your intuition! Pay heed to your intellect! Cultivate the concept from within your heart! Allow your thoughts to cascade like a fluid; there are no bounds, so unleash your creativity, draw inspiration, and seek out opportunities. The essence lies in recognising gaps and devising straightforward solutions.

Journey to Success

Concentrate on establishing yourself as a brand that delivers distinctive value to both you and your customers, effectively nullifying competition by generating demand and increasing credibility and positioning.

It is best to avoid cannibalisation within the chaos of the competition. Focus must remain to emerge as a unique preposition of products or services with value addition.

Create each interaction as a unique and smooth experience. This allows the customers to take pride in associating with the brand. Rest becomes history!

01

Strategy

Strategy is the blueprint that connects vision with actions.

It shapes the path to success with clarity, adaptability, and foresight.

- PREEA V MANE

Strategic Foundation

Strategy is a formulated plan, approach, or sequence of steps aimed at attaining a particular objective or outcome.

-Henry Mintzbery from MCGill University defines strategy in multiple definitions:

- Strategy as a pattern in a stream of decisions to contrast with a view of strategy as planning;

- Strategy as plan – a directed course of action to achieve an *intended* set of goals; similar to the strategic planning concept;

- Strategy as pattern – a consistent pattern of past behavior, with a strategy *realized* over time rather than planned or intended. Where the realized pattern was different from the intent, he referred to the strategy as emergent;

- Strategy as position – locating brands, products, or companies within the market, based on the conceptual framework of consumers or other stakeholders; a strategy determined primarily by factors outside the firm;

- Strategy as ploy – a specific maneuver intended to outwit a competitor; and

- Strategy as perspective – executing strategy based on a "theory of the business" or natural extension of the mindset or ideological perspective of the organization

Complexity theorists define strategy as the unfolding of the internal and external aspects of the organisation that result in actions in a socio-economic context.

In my view, when a sailor finds themselves amidst the vast expanse of the ocean, steering towards a predetermined destination, their reliance is solely on a fundamental tool "the magnetic compass". This indispensable instrument aids the sailor in navigating towards their intended destination.

Just as a magnetic compass guides a sailor towards their destination, so does a well-crafted strategy navigate us towards achieving our long-term vision and goals. Whether applied to personal aspirations or within the corporate realm, strategy expedites goal attainment in a systematic manner.

Join me in this edition as we focus on "Strategy for the corporate world." Before delving into strategy formulation, take time to meditate and clear your mind. With a serene mindset, let's embark on this journey akin to a sailor, ensuring preparedness for unforeseen crises such as market fluctuations, evolving government policies, and other unexpected challenges.

Remember the world is not perfect and neither are we.

What is important to remember is to preempt, adapt and change the direction if need be to reach the goal.

Design a solution for challenges to achieve the aim or goal.

Let's explore the distinctions among fundamental strategies to bring clarity to our minds as we embark on the **journey of strategising.**

Corporate Strategy guides us in understanding our position within the broader industry landscape and how we should position ourselves for competition. Decisions in this realm encompass diversification, vertical integration, acquisitions, new ventures, and resource allocation among different business units.

Business strategies, on the other hand, are centred on our business's ultimate objectives. Here, we define our competitive advantage through our value proposition, determining whether to introduce new products or services regardless of industry norms. We engage in ideation and innovation to stay ahead of competitors while meeting stakeholders' expectations.

Operational/Functional Strategy sets the overall direction, scope, and methodology for day-to-day operations, offering clarity on responsibilities and timelines while maintaining a focus on the market, competitive positioning, and resource management.

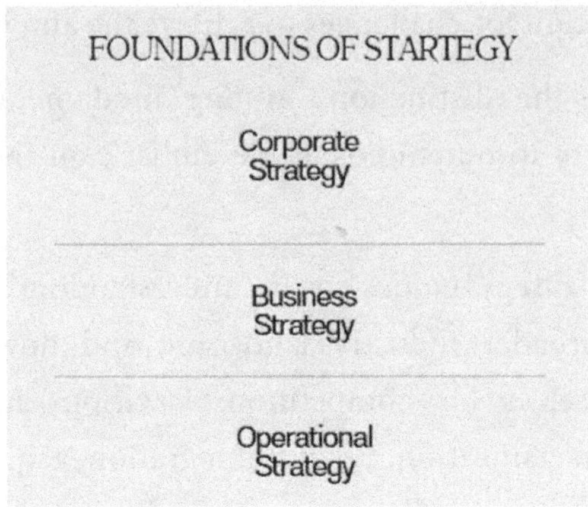

Importance of Strategy

Strategy serves as a cornerstone in establishing a distinct and valuable market position for a company.

Clear Roadmap: A robust strategy provides not only a roadmap but also the guiding principles and detailed instructions necessary for achieving the company's objectives.

How Strategy Helps? Startegy helps in:

- **Creation of a Unique and Valuable Position, identification and price positioning:**
  - ○ **Positioning:** Understanding the essence of packaging offerings differently from competitors to gain a competitive advantage.
  - ○ **Identification:** Identifying the target customer segment and devising accessible means to reach them through various channels.

- o **Price Positioning:** Determining pricing strategies based on the niche and customer segment, either pricing higher for overserved customers or competitively pricing for underserved ones.

- **Creation of Trade-offs in Competition to Determine What Not to Pursue:**

  - o **Trade-offs:** Establishing activities that are incompatible with competitors' strategies to maintain a sustainable competitive advantage.

  - o **Innovation and Simplicity:** Continuously evolving through innovation while keeping operations simple to avoid straying from core offerings.

  - o **Need for Choice:** Trade-offs necessitate making choices that protect against competitors' attempts to copy or reposition themselves.

- **Achievement of Sustainable Competitive Advantage:**

  - o **Reinforcement of Company Identity:** Integrating activities that complement each other to create real economic value and sustain competitive advantage.

  - o **Technological Integration:** Incorporating technologies to configure and integrate activities for consistent performance and output.

  - o **Organisational Alignment:** Aligning organisational structure with long-term strategic goals to enhance

> sustainability and achieve complementarities.
>
> o **Continual Improvement:** Fostering a culture of continuous improvement to reinforce the company's identity and sustain competitive advantage over time.

Micheal E. Porter states companies that try to be all things to all customers, in contrast, risk confusion in the trenches as employees attempt to make day-to-day operating decisions without a clear framework. False trade-offs between cost and quality occur primarily when there is redundant or wasted effort, poor control or accuracy, or weak coordination. Simultaneous improvement of cost and differentiation is possible only when a company begins far behind the productivity frontier or when the frontier shifts outward. At the frontier, where companies have achieved current best practices, the trade-off between cost and differentiation is very real indeed.

Michael E. Porter emphasises the risk of confusion when companies attempt to cater to all customer needs without a clear strategic framework. False trade-offs between cost and quality occur when efforts are redundant or poorly coordinated. Sustainable competitive advantage is achieved by reinforcing activities that competitors cannot easily replicate.

In my view, **"keeping it simple"** is the key. A clear vision, mission, and the smart creation and implementation of strategies not only keep employees focused but also enable them to deliver, and perhaps even exceed, expectations. This ultimately yields benefits and profitability for stakeholders, fostering a sense of pride among employees in their association with the company.

I see this as a win-win scenario for all stakeholders. Investors reap the rewards of profitability and credibility, customers enjoy high-quality products and services, and employees thrive in a stress-free environment with a focused approach. Their ability to exceed expectations boosts confidence and enhances their sense of belonging.

The Key Takeaway here is that, rather than comparing yourself to competitors, aim to make competition inconsequential by offering unparalleled value to both you and your customers. Elevate above the norm by providing a distinctive value proposition, rendering competitors irrelevant and positioning your strategy as the benchmark for others to emulate.

"Redefine Competition by Elevating, Excelling, and Inspiring."

–PREEA V MANE

Technology

The ever-evolving landscape of technology, characterised by advancements in Blockchain, Web3, and A.I., exerts a profound influence on the strategic direction and operational dynamics of businesses across all sectors, whether large or small, encompassing education, healthcare, agriculture, aerospace, and beyond. Leveraging simplified yet robust technological solutions is paramount to achieving success and satisfying both internal and external stakeholders.

Identifying and effectively allocating resources to the right technologies is crucial, as it enables organisations to enhance efficiency, foster agility, and deliver superior service to customers. This strategic approach not only cultivates a competitive edge but also facilitates the attainment of business objectives.

The Key Takeaways here are:

- **Automation:** Seamless integration of technology throughout all stages of operations, from foundational strategies to departmental processes and end-user experiences, is pivotal for optimising business outcomes and reinforcing brand positioning. By minimising manual interventions and labour, organisations can enhance efficiency, accuracy, and alignment with strategic objectives, ultimately bolstering stakeholder, shareholder, and customer satisfaction.

- **Data Analysis:** Embracing technology-driven solutions facilitates comprehensive data analysis, empowering businesses to harness vast datasets and present insights in a focused manner. This enables informed decision-making practices, enables performance tracking, identifies gaps, and fosters a culture of data-driven decision-making.

Navigating Transformation

A Journey in Real Estate Management Digitization

Embarking on a transformative journey in real estate management, I am eager to recount my experience in digitising end to end processes for smooth customer experience. Over a span of 15 months, I was deeply involved in this initiative, witnessing its profound impact on our organisation.

Background: Initially, our company grappled with inefficiencies due to the absence of established processes and employee policies. This led to a chaotic work environment characterised by confusion and blame-shifting. Leveraging my background in quality management, I recognised the pressing need for structured processes and digitisation to drive organisational excellence.

Initiatives: With steadfast support from our leadership, I collaborated with various departments and our esteemed Business Excellence team to formulate a comprehensive digital transformation strategy. A key component was reimagining our Human Capital department, underscoring the invaluable role of employees as assets to the organisation.

Centralisation: A pivotal aspect of our strategy was consolidating our operations from multiple city locations into a cohesive entity. This alignment fostered unity and facilitated a concerted approach towards our collective goals.

Digital Processes: Central to our transformation was the implementation of robust digital processes aimed at enhancing efficiency and client satisfaction. Through collaboration with I.T. and project management teams, we translated our vision into tangible solutions, empowering stakeholders with the necessary tools and resources.

Challenges and Successes: Our journey was not without challenges, yet through perseverance and collaboration, we navigated complexities and emerged stronger. The adoption of digital tools revolutionised our operations and elevated client relationships to new heights.

Outcomes: From streamlining workflows to ensuring compliance, our digital initiatives drove sustainable growth and fostered a culture of continuous improvement. Providing senior management with comprehensive insights enabled informed decision-making and staying ahead of the curve.

Brand Positioning

Brand positioning is the strategy of creating a distinct and valued place in the minds of consumers for a brand relative to its competitors. It involves highlighting unique features, benefits, and values that differentiate the brand, making it more appealing to the target audience.

- **Emotional Connection:**

  Emotions serve as a powerful catalyst for building profound and enduring bonds with customers. By crafting genuine experiences that resonate deeply with their hearts and emotions, brands can cultivate loyalty and advocacy. Establishing an emotional connection with the audience is essential for fostering lasting relationships and creating a sense of belonging.

- **Experiential Brand Positioning:**

  While technological advancements are important, human touch and emotional experiences remain fundamental human needs. Recognising this, brands must cultivate distinctive personalities with charismatic attitudes that evoke positive emotional responses. Emotional branding plays a pivotal role in prioritising the customer experience, thereby shaping the brand's identity and fostering customer loyalty.

- **Price Positioning:**

In the eyes of customers, value and experience often outweigh cost considerations. Customers are willing to pay a premium for products or services that offer substantial value and enhance their overall experience. Price becomes less of a primary factor in decision-making when customers perceive significant value and emotional connection with a brand.

- **Reduced Churn:**

Consistently delivering value and exceptional customer service at every touchpoint of the brand journey reduces the likelihood of customers switching to competitors. By creating memorable experiences throughout the customer relationship journey, businesses can minimise churn, maximise retention, and drive new sales through referrals.

- **Brand Influence:**

Brand influence manifests in various forms, from individuals proudly associating themselves with a brand to professional influencers endorsing it. Some brands hold emotional influence through their dedication to social causes, while others elevate status or fulfil specific needs. Regardless of the form, brand influence motivates customers to engage with the brand and fosters a sense of belonging or aspiration.

In my opinion, the quality and customer satisfaction should never be compromised. In today's dynamic landscape, where new brands emerge frequently and customer loyalty evolves rapidly, investing in informed decisions for brand positioning is paramount. This investment involves resources such as marketing, manpower, tools, and time, but it is crucial for securing customer loyalty and long-term success in a competitive market.

"Secure Success by investing wisely in Brand Positioning."

–PREEA V MANE

The Strategic Framework

Business strategy is the compass guiding organisational success, from conceptualising product designs to nurturing cohesive teamwork.

It's the thread weaving through corporate, business, and functional levels, ensuring alignment with strategic objectives and fostering collaboration at every turn.

Like a beacon in the fog, it illuminates the path from lofty aspirations to tangible achievements.

Business strategy serves as a vital tool in achieving organisational goals, offering guiding principles that inform numerous decisions ranging from product design to personnel management. It functions as a framework supporting management in the development and execution of plans aligned with strategic objectives. This framework ensures seamless operations across various levels of the organisation, fostering cohesion and collaboration among employees.

- **Corporate Level Strategy:**

  Sitting atop the planning pyramid, corporate-level strategy provides a comprehensive framework and direction for the organisation's journey. Formulated by top management, including board members, investors, and C-suite executives, this strategy encompasses expansion plans, mergers and acquisitions, diversification, and new investment areas. It considers the impact on every facet of the organisation, charting a path toward planned destinations.

- **Business Level Strategy:**

At the business level, general managers translate corporate-level directives into actionable goals closely tied to organisational mission. This strategy aligns with corporate objectives, focusing on achieving specific business outcomes. For example, if the corporate strategy aims to expand operations, the business-level strategy may involve rebranding the offerings to target new demographics.

- **Functional Level Strategy:**

At the functional level, business-level strategies are translated into actionable directives that define roles and responsibilities within specific functions or departments. Supervisors and line managers allocate larger projects into smaller tasks, tailoring directives to individual employees' skills and qualifications. This ensures alignment with broader organisational objectives while maximising employee contributions.

In essence, business strategy operates as a guiding beacon, directing organisational efforts from top-level aspirations to detailed functional tasks, ultimately driving the organisation toward its desired outcomes.

*"Navigate Success by letting
Business Strategy Be Your Guiding Beacon."*

−PREEA V MANE

Key Components of an Effective Business Strategy

The following elements are essential for constructing a robust business strategy:

- **Business Objective:** Your business objective or mission statement sets the course for the company, aligning the business strategy with the overarching vision. It should be translated into a detailed action plan, providing clear instructions on how to achieve organisational goals.

- **Core Values:** Business strategy must resonate with the core values of the organisation, establishing clear guidelines for behavior and decision-making. Articulating these values fosters a sense of accountability among colleagues, ensuring alignment with the organisation's standards.

- **SWOT Analysis:** SWOT analysis, encompassing Strengths, Weaknesses, Opportunities, and Threats, offers a snapshot of the company's current position. This analysis is integral to business strategy, enabling the identification of key areas and preparation for unforeseen challenges. It highlights strengths to leverage and weaknesses to address.

- **Operational Tactics:** Operational tactics involve translating vision and plans into actionable steps. Following the identification of resources through SWOT analysis, allocation and prioritisation of tasks become crucial. This approach aids in the efficient management of time and resources.

- **Measurement:** Incorporating mechanisms for tracking performance is essential for evaluating the effectiveness of the business strategy. Breaking down objectives into smaller, measurable targets allows for regular monitoring and assessment of progress.

These components collectively form the foundation of a well-crafted business strategy, guiding the organisation towards its desired outcomes.

In other words,

- Business Objective is defined as a clear mission statement guiding the direction of the company by translating the business strategy into actionable steps to achieve organisational goals.

- Core Values has to be aligned to ensure alignment with the organisation's core values by communicating clearly articulated values to encourage accountability among colleagues.

- Carry out SWOT Analysis

  - Strengths: Identify internal strengths to leverage.

  - Weaknesses: Recognise internal weaknesses to be addressed.

  - Opportunities: Explore external opportunities for growth.

  - Threats: Mitigate external threats to the business.

- Turn vision and plans into actionable tactics by allocating and prioritising resources efficiently based on SWOT analysis.

- Manage time and resources effectively to achieve strategic objectives.

- Incorporate mechanisms to monitor and evaluate performance.

- Break down objectives into smaller, measurable targets for regular assessment.

These components form the backbone of a successful business strategy, guiding the organisation towards its goals and ensuring long-term success.

The optimal time to prioritise business strategy!

When should you prioritise your business strategy? Investing in a solid business strategy is advantageous as it prompts intentional reflection on business operations. This becomes especially critical during pivotal transitions, such as launching a new venture, divesting an existing enterprise, or pursuing investment opportunities. Business strategies play a pivotal role in optimising returns and seizing market advantages during these significant shifts.

Moreover, business strategy is not solely about growth; it also serves to fully exploit available market opportunities. It's prudent to focus on refining your business strategy when venturing into new markets, seeking financial backing, restructuring your operations, or navigating substantial internal changes such as organisational restructuring or staffing adjustments. By aligning your strategy with these strategic initiatives, you can effectively navigate transitions and position your business for long-term success.

Strategic Business Initiatives for Competitive Advantage

- **Product Differentiation:** Elevating Brand Recognition by innovating and emphasising superior technology, pricing, features, or design, businesses set themselves apart from competitors. This strategy fosters brand loyalty as customers value the unique offerings of the brand.

- **Enhancing Customer Experience by reputation Building:** Businesses prioritise continuous improvement in customer service, aiming to enhance satisfaction and loyalty. Strategic initiatives focus on upscaling services and optimising online call centre efficiency to elevate the overall customer experience.

- **Targeting a Younger Market as Long-Term Brand Association:** Recognising the value of capturing young customers, organisations invest in engaging with this demographic to establish enduring brand loyalty. Acquiring a younger market not only expands the brand's presence but also cultivates future customer relationships.

- **Effective Pricing Strategy via lense of Perception Management:** Pricing strategies significantly influence customer perceptions of a business. Offering affordable pricing attracts new customers, while premium pricing adds aspirational value to the brand. Each pricing approach necessitates distinct business tactics, with low-priced models requiring higher sales volumes for profitability and premium pricing maintaining product exclusivity and profitability.

- **Commitment to Sustainability and meeting Market Demand:** Responding to increasing environmental consciousness, businesses implement sustainable practices to align with consumer values. Positioning the organisation as socially responsible fosters trust and integrity while addressing environmental concerns through initiatives like energy reduction and recycling programs.

- **Cross-Selling Initiatives to maximise customer value:** Some organisations focus on upselling additional products to existing customers, reducing customer acquisition costs and marketing expenditures. By expanding the range of products offered to each customer, businesses enhance revenue streams and customer lifetime value.

Understanding the Distinctions: Business Strategy, Business Plan, and Business Model

All three components—Business Strategy, Business Plan, and Business Model—are indispensable for a business's success and sustainability. Despite their interconnectedness, aspiring business strategists often confuse these concepts, particularly during interviews. Here's a detailed breakdown of their key differences:

- **Business Strategy:**

    o **Purpose:** Outlines the long-term vision and direction of the organisation, focusing on overarching goals, target markets, competitive advantages, and high-level tactics for success.

    o **Timeframe:** Long-term, spanning several years or decades.

    o **Components:** Market analysis, competitive analysis, value proposition, differentiation strategy, and strategic goals.

    o **Flexibility:** Highly adaptable to changing market conditions.

- **Business Plan:**

    o **Purpose:** Serves as a roadmap for achieving short-term and medium-term goals, breaking down strategy into actionable plans, including marketing strategies, operational plans, financial projections, and resource allocation.

- ○ **Timeframe:** Outlines the long-term vision and direction of the organisation.

- ○ **Components:** Executive summary, company description, marketing analysis, marketing plan, financial projections, and implementation timeline.

- ○ **Specificity:** Detailed, specific, and less flexible compared to the business strategy.

- **Business Model:**

  - ○ **Purpose:** Explains the fundamental logic of how the business operates and generates revenue, considering key components like customer segments, value propositions, revenue streams, channels, key resources, essential activities, main partnerships, customer relationships, and cost structure.

  - ○ **Timeframe:** Remains relatively stable over time.

  - ○ **Components:** Customer segments, value propositions, revenue streams, channels, key resources, essential activities, main partnerships, customer relationships, and cost structure.

In essence, while business strategy sets the long-term vision and direction, the business plan breaks it down into actionable plans for short and medium terms, and the business model explains how the business operates and generates revenue. Understanding the distinctions among these components is crucial for effective business planning and execution.

Evaluating Strategy Success: Key Metrics for Performance Assessment

Measuring the success of a business strategy is paramount, especially when it directly contributes to growth and enhances competitive or financial performance. Here's a detailed breakdown of how to gauge the effectiveness of your strategic plan:

- **Key Performance Indicators (KPIs) for Objective Achievement:**

  - **Sales Revenue:** Assess the overall revenue generated from sales activities.

  - **Number of Customers:** Track the total number of customers acquired or retained.

  - **Repeat Customer Sales:** Measure the percentage of sales generated from repeat customers.

  - **Customer Retention Rate:** Evaluate the percentage of customers retained over a specific period.

  - **Conversion Rate:** Monitor the percentage of leads converted into customers.

  - **Average Order Value:** Determine the average value of each customer transaction.

  - **Business Volume:** Measure the total volume of business activities conducted.

- **Competitive Position Assessment:**

  - **Market Share:** Determine the percentage of total market sales captured by the business.

  - **Market Position:** Evaluate the position of the business relative to competitors in the market.

  - **Sales Win Rate:** Measure the percentage of sales opportunities won by the business.

  - **Brand Awareness & Press Mentions:** Assess the level of brand recognition and media coverage.

  - **Margin Position vs Industry Average:** Compare the profit margins of the business with industry benchmarks.

  - **Sales Growth vs Industry Average:** Analyse the growth rate of sales compared to industry standards.

- **Financial Performance Measurement:**

  - **Gross Profit:** Calculate the total revenue minus the cost of goods sold.

  - **Net Profit:** Determine the total revenue minus all expenses, including taxes.

  - **Operating Profit:** Assess the profit generated from core business operations.

  - **EBIT and EBITDA:** Evaluate earnings before interest, taxes, depreciation, and amortisation.

○ **Return on Assets:** Measure the profitability of assets invested in the business.

○ **Free Cash Flow and Operating Cash Flow:** Evaluate the cash generated by the business after expenses and investments.

By monitoring these key metrics, businesses can effectively evaluate the success of their strategic plans and make informed decisions to drive continuous improvement and growth.

Strategy Management and Implementation

This section delves into the critical aspects of Strategy Management and Implementation, exploring the intricacies involved in formulating, executing, and monitoring strategic initiatives within an organisation. It emphasises the strategic planning process, from the initial conception of strategic objectives to the practical implementation of strategies to achieve organisational goals. This section provides insights into various strategic management frameworks and methodologies, equipping readers with the tools and techniques necessary to navigate the complexities of strategic decision-making. Additionally, it discusses the role of leadership in driving strategic initiatives forward, highlighting the importance of effective leadership in aligning organisational efforts with strategic objectives. Through real-world examples and case studies, this section offers practical guidance on how to overcome challenges and maximise the effectiveness of strategic management and implementation processes.

Importance of Strategy Management

Understanding Strategy Management and Implementation is crucial for effective organisational planning and execution.

- **Framework:** Strategy furnishes a framework for navigating the complexities of the external landscape, enabling informed decision-making, and fostering long-term success.

- **Direction and Clarity:** It aids in defining the organisation's mission, vision, and values, offering a clear sense of direction and purpose. This ensures alignment across the organisation, with everyone working towards common objectives.

- **Goal Consistency:** By aligning activities and resources with overarching business goals, it ensures that efforts are synchronised towards achieving shared objectives.

- **Efficient Resource Allocation:** It facilitates the effective allocation of resources, including financial, human, and technological assets, to maximise value contribution towards strategic objectives.

- **Adaptability to Change:** Strategic management empowers organisations to proactively anticipate and adapt to changes in the external environment. By implementing mechanisms for change anticipation, organisations can minimise the impact of uncertainties in the dynamic business landscape.

- **Competitive Edge:** By identifying unique strengths and capabilities, strategic management assists in crafting and executing effective strategies. This can lead to the development of a sustainable competitive advantage that sets the organisation apart from competitors.

- **Risk Mitigation:** Strategic management involves the assessment of potential risks and uncertainties in the business environment, aiming to mitigate risks and enhance resilience to unforeseen challenges.

Mastering Strategy Implementation: The Key to Sustained Competitive Advantage

The significance of implementing a strategy cannot be overstated. While a well-crafted and straightforward strategy may establish your presence in the competitive landscape, its robust execution maintains your position. Effective strategy implementation starts with educating those responsible for carrying it out. Guiding management and implementation efforts aim to realise objectives aligned with strategic planning. This involves managing resources efficiently, continually refining internal processes, and adapting to external influences. By formulating action plans, businesses prepare themselves for competition, identify opportunities, and mitigate risks, thereby gaining a competitive advantage in dynamic market conditions.

Unlocking Success: The Strategic Management Journey

Strategic management encompasses a series of crucial steps that guide organisations towards their long-term goals. At the outset, establishing strategic direction is paramount, which involves defining the organisation's vision, mission, and overarching goals. This provides a clear sense of purpose and direction, aligning all efforts towards a common objective.

Following this, strategic management delves into analysing the internal and external factors through tools like SWOT analysis, identifying strengths, weaknesses, opportunities, and threats. Based on this analysis, corporate-level and business-level strategies are formulated, outlining the broad framework and specific tactics to achieve strategic objectives. Strategic planning further solidifies these strategies, detailing the actions required for implementation.

Strategic implementation involves translating plans into action, encompassing various aspects such as project management, procedural adjustments, resource allocation, structural changes, and behavioural adaptations within the organisation. This stage is crucial for executing the strategies effectively and efficiently, ensuring that the intended outcomes are achieved.

Finally, strategic evaluation becomes imperative to assess the effectiveness of the strategies implemented. This involves continuous analysis and assessment of performance metrics, comparing actual outcomes with desired objectives, and making necessary adjustments to optimise strategic efforts. Through strategic evaluation, organisations can learn from their experiences, refine their approaches, and enhance their overall strategic management processes.

The Strategic Management Process: A Roadmap to Success

- **Strategic Direction:**

    o **Vision, Mission, and Goals:** Establish a clear sense of purpose and direction for the organisation by defining its long-term vision, mission statement, and overarching goals.

- **Strategic Analysis:**

  - ○ **SWOT Analysis:** Evaluate the internal strengths and weaknesses as well as external opportunities and threats to inform strategic decision-making.

  - ○ **Environmental Scan:** Conduct a comprehensive analysis of the business environment, including market trends, competitor activities, and regulatory factors.

- **Strategy Formulation:**

  - ○ **Corporate Level Strategy:** Determine the overall scope and direction of the organisation, including decisions related to diversification, mergers, and acquisitions.

  - ○ **Business Level Strategy:** Develop strategies tailored to specific business units or product lines, focusing on competitive positioning and value creation.

  - ○ **Strategic Planning:** Translate strategic goals into actionable plans, outlining the resources, activities, and timelines required for implementation.

- **Strategy Implementation:**

  - ○ **Project Management:** Execute strategic initiatives through well-defined project plans, including task allocation, budgeting, and timeline management.

o **Procedural Adjustments:** Modify organisational processes and procedures to align with strategic objectives and enhance operational efficiency.

o **Resource Allocation:** Allocate resources such as finances, manpower, and technology to support strategic initiatives and maximise their impact.

o **Structural Changes:** Implement organisational restructuring or realignment to streamline operations and improve decision-making processes.

o **Behavioural Adaptations:** Foster a culture of strategic alignment and accountability, encouraging employees to embrace change and contribute to strategic goals.

- **Strategic Evaluation:**

  o **Analysis and Assessments:** Continuously monitor and evaluate the progress of strategic initiatives, analysing key performance indicators and benchmarking against predefined targets.

  o **Feedback and Learning:** Solicit feedback from stakeholders, learn from successes and failures, and adapt strategies accordingly to enhance effectiveness and agility.

The strategic management process serves as a roadmap for organisations to navigate complex business environments, achieve their long-term objectives, and sustain competitive advantage. By following these key steps—from defining strategic direction to implementing and evaluating strategies—organisations can proactively respond to challenges, capitalise on opportunities, and drive sustainable growth.

The Vital Role of Business Excellence and Risk Analysis

- **Importance of Business Excellence & Risk Analysis:** Business excellence and risk analysis serve as the nervous system of an organisation, ensuring that it operates effectively and proactively addresses potential threats.

- **Analogous to the Nervous System:** Just as the nervous system regulates and responds to signals in the human body, business excellence and risk analysis provide indicators and warnings that prompt timely action and preventive measures.

- **Components of Business Excellence & Risk Analysis:**

  o **Strategic Mapping:** Utilising strategic mapping processes to align business objectives and identify potential risks.

  o **Scorecards:** Implementing scorecards to measure performance and identify areas for improvement.

  o **Delegation of Authority:** Establishing clear lines of authority and responsibility to ensure accountability.

  o **Technology Implementation:** Leveraging

cutting-edge technology to enhance efficiency and effectiveness.

- o **Group-Level Assessments:** Conduct thorough assessments at the group level to identify the root causes of issues and anticipate future challenges.

- **Benefits of Business Excellence & Risk Analysis:**

  - o **Proactive Problem-Solving:** Enables organisations to anticipate and prevent problems before they occur.

  - o **Continual Process Improvements:** Facilitates ongoing enhancements to processes, leading to greater efficiency and effectiveness.

  - o **Damage Mitigation:** Helps in mitigating potential damages by addressing issues in their early stages.

  - o **Strategic Decision-Making:** Provides valuable insights for strategic decision-making and resource allocation.

In summary, Business excellence and risk analysis are integral components of strategic management, ensuring that organisations operate optimally and are well-prepared to navigate challenges and seize opportunities in an ever-evolving business landscape.

Elevating Profitability through Operations Management

Operations management plays a pivotal role in maintaining

superior profitability by emphasising continuous improvement, consistency, and efficiency in operational effectiveness. It adopts a highly quantitative approach aimed at striking a balance between costs and revenue to maximise net operating profit. This multifaceted discipline encompasses various aspects such as inventory management, supply chain optimisation, delivery logistics, and manufacturing plant operations. Effective operations management involves meticulous oversight of factors like plant size, capacity utilisation, delivery output, and budget management. The focus remains on minimising costs while optimising revenue streams to ensure high profit margins for the organisation. In essence, operations management is a structured and data-driven strategy designed to enhance overall profitability through streamlined processes and resource utilisation.

- **Operations Management:**

Operations management is a systematic approach to overseeing various operational activities within an organisation to ensure efficiency and maximise profitability. Key Components are Inventory management, supply chain optimisation, delivery logistics, manufacturing plant operations.

- **Goals of Operations Management:**

  - **Continuous Improvement:** Striving for ongoing enhancements in processes and procedures to boost efficiency and effectiveness.

  - **Consistency:** Maintaining a uniform level of

performance to deliver quality products or services consistently.

- **Speed:** Focusing on swift and timely execution of tasks to meet customer demands and market expectations.

- **Strategies for Profitability:**

  - **Cost Optimisation:** Balancing costs with revenue to achieve the highest possible net operating profit.

  - **Revenue Enhancement:** Implementing strategies to increase revenue streams while maintaining healthy profit margins.

  - **Margin Maximization:** Keeping costs low and revenues high to ensure optimal profitability.

- **Benefits of Effective Operations Management:**

  - **Increased Profitability:** By optimising resources and processes, organisations can achieve higher levels of profitability.

  - **Competitive Advantage:** Efficient operations provide a competitive edge by offering better products or services at lower costs.

  - **Enhanced Customer Satisfaction:** Streamlined operations lead to improved product quality, timely deliveries, and better customer service.

Operations management is essential for businesses seeking to maximise profitability by optimising resources, minimising costs, and delivering superior products or services. By adopting effective strategies and practices, organisations can achieve sustainable growth and success in today's competitive market landscape.

Optimising Success Through Strategic Manpower Management

The success of any strategy hinges upon having the right manpower in place. I've observed businesses falter due to demotivated and misaligned employees. Thus, securing and effectively managing manpower is vital for fostering engagement, productivity, and loyalty. Despite the rise of technology and its impact on job displacement, the human touch remains paramount, especially in customer service and experience. To simplify this complex topic, let's focus on key themes.

Attracting and retaining talent, aligning employees with evolving strategies, and promoting continual growth are pivotal for organisational success. Companies that integrate human capital planning with sustainable development goals yield broader positive impacts. Ensuring roles match skill sets and fostering self-motivated individuals with a positive, learning-oriented attitude is crucial for steering the company toward its future goals.

Human capital function plays a critical role in shaping the employee experience, fostering integrity, inclusivity, skill-building, social mentoring, and engagement. It involves implementing programs for continual learning, upskilling, transparent communication, and leadership development. Human resource strategy focuses on optimising talent attraction, retention, and motivation, while people strategy centres on enhancing human performance to impact the organisation's bottom line.

The aim of human resource strategy is to align skills and goals with business objectives through concrete measures, programs, and key performance indicators (KPIs). Strategic manpower management within people strategy involves creating a coherent framework for hiring, managing, and developing employees to support the organisation's long-term goals.

Unlocking Success: Strategic Manpower Management

Strategic manpower management is crucial for organisational success. It involves attracting, retaining, and aligning talent with business goals.

- **Importance of Human Capital:**
    - Human capital shapes the employee experience and organisational culture.
    - Key aspects include skill-building, engagement, and continual learning.

- **Human Resource Strategy:**
    - Focuses on optimising talent attraction, retention, and motivation.
    - Concrete measures, programs, and KPIs are implemented to align skills with business objectives.

- **People Strategy:**
    - Aims to enhance human performance to impact the organisation's bottom line.

- o Involves coherent frameworks for hiring, managing, and developing employees.

- **Core Components:**

  - o Role alignment, skill matching, and fostering a positive, learning-oriented attitude.

  - o Programs for continual learning, upskilling, and leadership development are vital.

- **Achieving Success:**

  - o Integration of human capital planning with sustainable development goals.

  - o Promotes inclusivity, transparency, and employee well-being.

Strategic manpower management is essential for driving organisational growth and success. By prioritising talent development and alignment, businesses can thrive in dynamic environments.

Navigating Technology Integration: A Strategic Approach

Implementing new technology requires careful planning and alignment across departments. Before initiating technology implementation, it's crucial to identify integrated processes and relevant departments. Leadership plays a pivotal role in setting the norm for technology adoption within the company. They must bring stakeholders together to ensure alignment and address any resistance strategically. Failure to manage resistance effectively can result in delays, impacting stakeholder journeys and overall productivity. Ignoring resistance management can lead to missed opportunities and financial losses. Therefore, proactive management of resistance is essential for successful technology implementation.

Navigating Technology Integration: A Strategic Approach

01 Understand Integration: Before implementing new technology, identify integrated processes and relevant departments.

02 Leadership Alignment: Leadership plays a crucial role in setting the norm for technology adoption within the company.

03 Stakeholder Alignment: Bring stakeholders together to ensure alignment and address any resistance strategically.

04 Resistance Management: Proactively manage resistance to prevent delays and ensure smooth implementation.

05 Impact of Ignorance: Ignoring resistance management can lead to missed opportunities and financial losses.

The Dynamic Framework of Balanced Scorecard

The Balanced Scorecard serves as the foundational DNA of organisational strategy, facilitating continual monitoring and evaluation across various perspectives. It encompasses financial, non-financial, customer relations, internal processes, and learning and growth aspects, aligning short-term actions with long-term strategic goals. Lets understand the benefit of application of the balance scorecard framework.

- **Real-Time Insights:** Provides real-time data for reporting to shareholders, boards, and stakeholders, enabling agile decision-making to steer the organisation in the right direction.

- **Strategic Understanding:** Empowers managers to ensure that all levels of the organisation comprehend and are aligned with the long-term strategy, fostering strategic clarity and coherence.

- **Focus and Alignment:** Establishes a framework that promotes focus in business planning, goal setting, capital allocation, and strategic initiatives, fostering alignment and accountability across departments and individuals.

- **Continuous Reference:** Serves as a readily available tool for reference at all levels of the organisation, ensuring consistent alignment with strategic objectives.

- **Measurement and Accountability:** Enables the measurement of progress and achievement toward key performance indicators, encompassing both financial and non-financial metrics, thus promoting accountability and driving performance improvement initiatives.

Unlocking Success: The Power of Balanced Scorecard

The Balanced Scorecard (BSC) is a strategic management framework that translates an organisation's mission and vision into actionable objectives and metrics across multiple perspectives like financial, customer, internal processes and learning and growth.

- **Perspectives:**

  - **Financial:** Monitor financial health and performance indicators such as revenue growth, profitability, and cost management.

  - **Customer:** Evaluate customer satisfaction, loyalty, and retention rates to ensure sustained business success.

  - **Internal Processes:** Optimise operational efficiency, quality, and innovation to drive organisational effectiveness.

  - **Learning and Growth:** Foster employee development, skills enhancement, and organisational learning to support long-term sustainability.

- **Key Features:**

  - **Comprehensive Measurement:** Track performance

across all perspectives to gain holistic insights into organisational health.

- ○ **Alignment:** Ensure alignment of individual and departmental goals with overall strategic objectives.

- ○ **Adaptability:** Enable real-time adjustments and strategic shifts in response to changing market dynamics.

- ○ **Accountability:** Hold stakeholders accountable for achieving targets and driving continuous improvement.

- **Benefits:**

  - ○ **Strategic Clarity:** Provide a clear roadmap for executing organisational strategy and achieving long-term goals.

  - ○ **Performance Improvement:** Drive performance enhancements by identifying areas for optimisation and innovation.

  - ○ **Stakeholder Communication:** Facilitate transparent communication with stakeholders through data-driven insights.

  - ○ **Competitive Advantage:** Gain a competitive edge by leveraging data-driven decision-making and strategic alignment.

- **Implementation Steps:**

  - **Define Objectives:** Clearly articulate strategic objectives and metrics for each perspective.

  - **Develop Measures:** Identify relevant KPIs and metrics to track progress and performance.

  - **Implement Initiatives:** Execute action plans and initiatives aligned with strategic objectives.

  - **Monitor and Review:** Continuously monitor performance, review results, and adjust strategies as needed.

Financial Navigation: The Symbiotic Relationship of Budgeting and Planning

Budgeting and planning are integral components of effective financial management, serving as interconnected exercises that drive growth, control, adaptation, and flexibility within an organisation. They work together to establish financial goals, allocate resources efficiently, manage expenses, maintain financial control, and adapt to changing financial circumstances, ultimately leading to the desired financial outcomes.

When implementing a strategy, it is crucial to align budgeting and planning to determine the timeframe for achieving strategic success. By aligning financial goals from both long-term and short-term strategies and regularly forecasting financial performance, organisations can navigate smoothly and provide shareholders and stakeholders with a realistic view of planned budgets versus actual achievements. Close monitoring of financial data allows for timely adjustments to strategic direction as needed.

The allocation of budget resources according to different financial priorities is essential for achieving desired financial growth. Close monitoring of actual spending and earnings is critical for accurate financial forecasting, focusing on metrics such as earnings before interest, taxes, depreciation, and amortisation (EBITDA). EBITDA serves as a valuable measure for investors and is used to benchmark a company's performance against its peers. However, it should be assessed alongside other key performance indicators such as operating income and net income.

Budgeting transforms financial forecasts into detailed plans for income allocation and expense management on a monthly or yearly basis. Planning identifies the appropriate allocation of funds across various areas, providing a framework for implementing these allocations on a day-to-day basis. Together, budgeting and planning ensure financial stability, efficiency, and strategic alignment within an organisation.

Budgeting and planning are essential components of effective financial management, working hand in hand to drive growth, control, adaptation, and flexibility within organisations.

- **Budgeting:**
    - Establishes financial goals.
    - Allocates resources efficiently.
    - Manages expenses effectively.
    - Maintains financial control.

- **Planning:**
    - Translates financial goals into detailed plans.
    - Identifies allocation of funds across various areas.
    - Provides a framework for day-to-day implementation.

- **Alignment with Strategy:**
    - Determines timeframe for achieving strategic success.

- o Aligns financial goals with long-term and short-term strategies.

- o Regularly forecasts financial performance for informed decision-making.

- **Monitoring and Adaptation:**

  - o Close monitoring of actual spending and earnings.

  - o Timely adjustments to strategic direction based on financial data.

  - o Ensures a realistic view of planned budgets versus actual achievements.

- **Key Metrics:**

  - o Earnings Before Interest, Taxes, Depreciation, and Amortization (EBITDA)

  - o Benchmark for company performance.

  - o Assessed alongside other key performance indicators.

Budgeting and planning are vital for financial stability, efficiency, and strategic alignment within organisations, driving them toward desired financial outcomes.

Cultivating Brand Loyalty: The Power of Customer Retention and Service

Customer retention and exceptional customer service play pivotal roles in fostering brand loyalty and ensuring sustained success and growth for businesses. Positive reinforcement, such as words of appreciation and social praise, triggers dopamine responses in customers, reinforcing their loyalty to the brand.

- **Brand Loyalty and Value Proposition:**

  Maintaining a strong brand positioning and delivering high-quality, experiential customer service is key to earning and retaining customer loyalty. This not only saves costs by avoiding the need to acquire new customers but also enhances brand authority with minimal investment.

- **Distinctive Value Proposition:**

  Customers remain loyal to brands that offer unique, relevant, and superior value propositions. Craftsmanship, heritage, and emotional benefits contribute to this value, fostering long-term brand loyalty that transcends generations.

- **Post-Purchase Experience:**

  Meeting or exceeding customer expectations leads to positive experiences, reducing post-purchase regret and solidifying brand loyalty.

- **Recurring Business and Referrals:**

  Consistently offering value builds trust and fosters long-term relationships, resulting in recurring business and positive word-of-mouth referrals, which are powerful marketing tools.

- **Customer-Centric Service and Brand Positioning:**

  Customer service excellence is achieved through a customer-centric focus aligned with brand positioning. Every interaction point with the brand should enhance the customer's experience, reflecting the company's culture and values at all levels.

- **Feedback Collection and Adaptation:**

  Opening feedback loops enables businesses to understand evolving customer preferences and refine offerings accordingly. This ensures continuous alignment with customer needs and preferences, enhancing long-term loyalty and satisfaction.

By prioritising customer retention, delivering exceptional service, and maintaining a strong brand identity, businesses can cultivate enduring brand loyalty, driving sustained success and growth.

02

Leadership

"Leadership combines strategy and character to turn vision into reality"

- PREEA V MANE

Leadership Dynamics

"Leadership encompasses both strategic acumen and personal character. Without character, even the most brilliant strategy may falter." – U.S. Gen. H. Norman Schwarzkopf emphasised the critical synergy between strategy and character ineffective leadership. Similarly, Warren G. Bennis, the founding chairman of the Leadership Institute at the University of Southern California, viewed leadership as the ability to translate vision into tangible outcomes, underscoring its transformative nature.

"Great leaders are adept at simplifying complexities and offering solutions that resonate with everyone." —Gen. Colin Powell highlighted the essence of simplicity in leadership, emphasising the importance of clarity amidst ambiguity. In essence, leadership involves inspiring and motivating teams to achieve success rooted in the embodiment of exemplary traits and behaviours. Leading by example is paramount, as leaders serve as the guiding force within an organisation.

Leadership serves as the cornerstone that fortifies organisational unity and coherence. The leadership style, actions, and values exhibited by leaders profoundly influence team culture and morale, subsequently impacting the organisation. Leaders wield influence by modelling desired behaviours, articulating core values, fostering trust, empowering teams, resolving conflicts, and cultivating a conducive work environment.

Ultimately, leadership is not merely a role but an attitude—a steadfast commitment to guiding and uplifting others toward shared goals and aspirations.

"Leadership is an attitude."

–PREEA V MANE

When we say, "leadership is an attitude," we're emphasising that leadership goes beyond just a set of skills or actions; it's a fundamental mindset that guides how individuals approach their roles and responsibilities. This perspective underscores the importance of adopting a proactive and empowered stance towards problem-solving, decision-making, and influencing others. In essence, it suggests that effective leadership stems from a deeply ingrained belief in one's ability to inspire, guide, and empower others towards shared goals. Leaders with this attitude are constantly seeking opportunities to lead by example, foster collaboration, and drive positive change within their teams and organisations. Leadership is not merely a title or position but a way of thinking and behaving that can inspire others to reach their full potential.

Cultivating Leadership in Supportive Environments

Leadership is not simply attained through rote learning but flourishes in environments that foster critical thinking, problem-solving, creativity, and adaptability. Central to this development is leadership by influence, where individuals are empowered to implement management concepts through practical application rather than mere memorisation of theories.

The ability to make effective decisions swiftly is paramount in distinguishing efficient management. Clear and decisive choices prevent system paralysis, alleviate workforce confusion, and catalyse organisational growth. However, maintaining balance and impartiality in decision-making processes is essential to mitigate biases and ensure equitable outcomes.

Jim Rohn's quote encapsulates the multifaceted nature of effective leadership, emphasising the importance of strength tempered by kindness, boldness tempered by thoughtfulness, and pride tempered by humility. This nuanced approach to leadership reflects a commitment to integrity, empathy, and ethical conduct in all endeavours.

Furthermore, self-awareness of one's strengths and weaknesses is instrumental in honing leadership skills. By leveraging strengths to excel in tasks and delegating areas of weakness to capable team members, leaders can optimise their effectiveness and foster a culture of collaboration and empowerment.

In essence, successful leadership thrives in environments that encourage growth, accountability, and authenticity. By cultivating a supportive culture that values innovation, continuous learning, and self-improvement, organisations can nurture the next generation of visionary leaders poised to navigate complex challenges and drive sustainable success.

Shaping Reality: The Power of Perception in Leadership

Perception plays a profound role in shaping our understanding of the world around us. Much like the age-old analogy of the glass being half empty or half full, our interpretation of situations can greatly influence our reality. This concept extends to leadership, where how others perceive a leader's abilities and effectiveness becomes their reality.

Consider the various perspectives on the glass analogy, from the optimist seeing the glass as half full to the engineer analysing its size relative to necessity. Each viewpoint offers a unique insight into how individuals process information through their own filters of experience, emotions, and beliefs.

Understanding this diversity in perception is crucial for leaders. By recognising the different lenses through which people perceive reality, leaders can tailor their communication and actions to effectively influence outcomes. This nuanced understanding enables leaders to build trust, foster collaboration, and drive meaningful change within their teams and organisations.

Leadership isn't about imposing one's will but rather about understanding and leveraging the multitude of perspectives to create a culture of inclusivity and innovation. By embracing this approach, leaders can cultivate environments where diverse viewpoints are valued and decisions are made collaboratively, leading to greater organisational success.

Understanding that perception shapes reality and the analogy of the glass half empty vs. half full is discussed in the following.

- **Different Perspectives on the Glass:**

  - **The Optimist:** Sees the glass as half full.

  - **The Pessimist:** Views the glass as half empty.

  - **The Salesperson:** Asks how much water the glass should hold.

  - **The accountant:** Questions the necessity of all the water.

  - **The Engineer:** Analyses the glass's size relative to its need.

  - **The Quantum Physicist:** Sees a 50% probability of holding water.

  - **The Philosopher:** Contemplates the perception of the glass when unobserved.

  - **The Politician:** Proposes taking a poll to determine the glass's status.

  - **The Servant Leader:** Prioritises using the water to quench others' thirsts.

- **Impact on Leadership:**

  - Perception of a leader's abilities shapes others' reality.

  - Understanding diverse perceptions is crucial for effective leadership.

  - Tailoring communication and actions to influence outcomes.

  - Building trust, fostering collaboration, and driving meaningful change.

  - Embracing diverse perspectives creates inclusive and innovative cultures.

  - Leadership is not about imposing one's will but about leveraging diverse viewpoints for success.

Leadership requires understanding and leveraging perception. Embrace diversity to create inclusive and innovative environments. Influence outcomes by recognising and respecting varied perspectives.

Navigating Success: The Importance of Vision and Mission Statements

Understanding a company's vision and mission statement is paramount for organisational success. These statements serve as guiding lights, illuminating the path toward achieving the company's goals and aspirations. A well-defined vision articulates the company's future state, outlining what it aims to achieve, while the mission statement delineates how it plans to reach those objectives. These statements provide a framework for decision-making, ensuring that all actions are aligned with the overarching goals of the organisation.

Moreover, vision and mission statements form the bedrock for strategic planning, laying the foundation for setting strategic objectives that support the organisation's mission. They serve as powerful communication tools, conveying the company's purpose, values, and goals to stakeholders both within and outside the organisation. By articulating a clear vision and mission, companies can attract like-minded customers, investors, and employees who share their values and vision.

Beyond mere communication, well-crafted vision and mission statements inspire and motivate stakeholders, instilling a sense of purpose and direction. They foster greater engagement, commitment, and productivity among employees by providing a unifying goal to strive toward. In essence, vision and mission statements are indispensable components of a clear and effective business strategy plan, offering direction, purpose, and motivation to propel the organisation toward success.

Charting a Course for Organizational Excellence

Importance of Vision and Mission:

- **Clarity:** Provides a clear understanding of the company's objectives and how to achieve them.

- o **Alignment:** Ensures that all actions and decisions are in line with overarching goals.

- o **Decision-making:** Guides strategic choices and resource allocation.

Building Blocks of Vision and Mission:

- o **Vision Statement:** Defines the company's future aspirations and desired outcomes.

- o **Mission Statement:** Articulates how the company will fulfil its vision and serve its stakeholders.

Strategic Planning and Execution:

- o **Framework:** Forms the foundation for developing strategic objectives and action plans.

- o **Communication:** Serves as a powerful tool for conveying purpose, values, and goals across the organisation.

Stakeholder Engagement and Alignment:

- o **Attraction:** Helps attract customers, investors, and employees who share similar values and vision.

- o **Inspiration:** Motivates and inspires stakeholders, fostering greater engagement and commitment.

Driving Organisational Success:

- **Direction:** Provides a roadmap for navigating challenges and seizing opportunities.

- **Purpose:** Instils a sense of purpose and meaning, driving employee productivity and organisational performance.

Vision and mission statements are essential elements of effective business strategy, offering direction, alignment, and inspiration for organisational success.

Norms and Organisational Culture: Shaping the Workplace Landscape

In every organisation, norms and culture play a pivotal role in shaping the workplace environment and influencing employee behaviour.

Norms represent the unwritten rules and expectations that guide interactions and behaviour within the organisation. These norms can range from basic etiquette to more complex social norms that govern how work is conducted and decisions are made. For example, a norm of punctuality may be established, encouraging employees to arrive on time for meetings and appointments.

Organisational culture, on the other hand, encompasses the shared values, beliefs, and practices that define the identity of the organisation. It reflects the collective mindset and behaviours of employees and leaders, influencing everything from communication styles to decision-making processes. A culture of innovation, for instance, may encourage risk-taking and experimentation to drive progress and growth.

Together, norms and culture create the fabric of the workplace, shaping interactions, attitudes, and outcomes. They provide a sense of identity and belonging for employees, fostering cohesion and alignment towards common goals.

Effective leaders recognise the importance of norms and culture in cultivating a positive work environment. By promoting values such as transparency, collaboration, and inclusivity, they can nurture a culture that empowers employees, promotes engagement, and drives organisational success.

In summary, norms and organisational culture are integral aspects of the workplace landscape, influencing behaviour, shaping identity, and driving performance.

Nurturing Company Culture: The Role of the Human Capital Team

The foundation of company norms often begins with the leader and is nurtured by the Human Capital Team. I prefer to refer to them as the Human Capital Team because their role extends beyond traditional H.R. functions; they strategically manage and develop the organisation's most asset - its people. Under the guidance of a leader who prioritises people-centric strategies and understands the significance of employees in driving organisational success, the Human Capital Team plays a crucial role in shaping the company culture and fostering an environment conducive to growth and innovation.

Their responsibilities include not only traditional H.R. tasks such as recruitment and employee relations but also strategic workforce planning, talent development, and fostering a culture of continuous learning and development. By leveraging initiatives such as networking events, personal and professional development programs, and skill-building workshops, the Human Capital Team fosters collaboration, enhances employee engagement, and cultivates a sense of belonging within the organisation. This proactive approach to human capital management ensures that employees are not only equipped with the skills and resources they need to succeed but also feel valued, supported, and motivated to contribute their best to the company's objectives.

I've observed firsthand a successful initiative within an organisation that propelled it towards becoming a publicly listed company. Under the guidance of a leader who prioritised people-focused strategies and recognised the crucial role employees play in organisational progress, the Human Resource department underwent a transformation. It was rebranded as "Human Capital", signifying a shift towards valuing employees as valuable assets.

The organisation was previously dispersed across multiple city locations with distinct brand positioning, but a shared objective was centralised under one operational umbrella. This consolidation facilitated cohesion and alignment towards common goals.

The Human Capital department was strategically aligned with long-term organisational objectives, playing a pivotal role in fostering a new organisational culture. Through various initiatives such as networking workshops, personal and professional development programs, and skill-building workshops, they fostered camaraderie among employees from diverse departments. This promoted better coordination and mutual understanding of strengths and challenges and cultivated an inclusive environment.

Leadership's Influence on Organisational Culture and Change

Gen. George S. Patton once remarked, "Never tell people how to do things. Tell them what to do, and they will surprise you with their ingenuity." This quote underscores the importance of leadership in fostering creativity and innovation within an organisation. Leaders not only guide the day-to-day operations but also shape the organisation's culture, norms, and values.

Effective leaders understand their role in creating an environment where employees feel empowered to showcase their ingenuity. By providing clear direction and goals, leaders allow employees to leverage their skills and creativity to achieve remarkable outcomes. This approach not only boosts morale but also fosters a culture of innovation and excellence.

Moreover, leaders are instrumental in managing change within the organisation. As the business landscape evolves, leaders must navigate transitions smoothly and minimise resistance to change. By communicating the rationale and objectives behind changes, providing reassurance, and offering support, leaders can instil trust and loyalty among employees. This, in turn, enhances productivity, accountability, and customer satisfaction.

In essence, leadership plays a pivotal role in shaping organisational culture and managing change effectively. Strong leadership ensures that the organisation remains adaptable, resilient, and poised for success amidst evolving challenges and opportunities.

Key Points can be summarized in a structured way

- **Inspiring Creativity:** Effective leadership empowers employees to showcase their ingenuity by providing clear direction and goals.

- **Shaping Organisational Culture:** Leaders play a crucial role in shaping the norms, values, and beliefs that define the organisation's culture.

- **Managing Change:** Leaders navigate transitions smoothly by communicating the rationale and objectives behind changes and offering support to employees.

- **Boosting Morale:** A culture of innovation and excellence fostered by leadership boosts employee morale and enhances productivity.

- **Driving Success:** Strong leadership ensures that the organisation remains adaptable, resilient, and poised for success amidst evolving challenges and opportunities.

Fostering a Positive Organizational Culture for Enhanced Employee Morale

- **Shared Leadership:** Leaders who work alongside their

teams and empower them to take ownership foster a sense of collective achievement, as illustrated by the quote from Lao Tzu.

- **Guiding Transformation:** Effective leaders guide their teams toward new horizons, as highlighted by Henry Kissinger's perspective on leadership.

- **Unleashing Greatness:** Leaders have the power to inspire greatness in their teams by recognising and eliciting their inherent potential, as emphasised by John Buchan.

- **Culture's Impact:** A strong organisational culture, characterised by shared values and behaviours, shapes the company's identity and influences employee interactions.

- **Employee Morale:** A thriving culture contributes to higher levels of morale, satisfaction, happiness, and motivation among employees, ultimately driving success and innovation.

Understanding the Dynamics of Power in Leadership

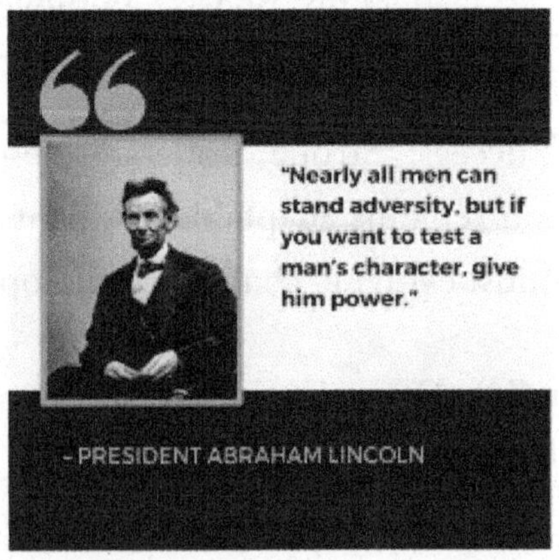

President Abraham Lincoln's quote highlights the true test of an individual's character when given power.

Power is the capacity to influence others' behaviour and persuade them to act in ways they might not otherwise.

McClelland's findings suggest that seeking and using power are inherent aspects of management that are necessary for effective leadership.

- **Types of Power:** Leaders wield various forms of power, including Reward, Legitimate, Referent, and Expert power.

- **Reward Power:** Involves incentivising behaviour through rewards such as praise, promotions, and desirable job assignments.

- **Legitimate Power:** Based on established norms and beliefs, certain individuals are granted the authority to govern or influence others.

- **Referent Power:** Also known as charismatic power, it arises from admiration and respect for an individual, influencing others to emulate their behaviour.

- **Expert Power:** Derives from possessing expertise, knowledge, or talent, allowing leaders to influence attitudes and behaviours through their expertise.

Power in leadership encompasses the ability to motivate, guide, and inspire others toward shared goals. While power can be a force for positive change and progress, it also presents challenges, as seen in President Lincoln's quote. McClelland's research sheds light on the nuanced role of power in management, emphasising its essential nature in organisational dynamics. Leaders leverage various forms of power strategically to influence individuals and teams, fostering collaboration, innovation, and growth. Understanding the dynamics of power is crucial for effective leadership, as it shapes organisational culture, employee engagement, and overall success.

Cultivating Employee Resilience for Organizational Success

In today's rapidly changing business landscape, the ability of employees to adapt, thrive, and remain productive amidst uncertainty is more critical than ever. At the heart of this resilience lies the organisational culture shaped by leaders. By fostering an environment of trust, belonging, and continuous learning, leaders lay the foundation for building employee resilience. This culture encourages employees to embrace change as an opportunity for growth and innovation rather than viewing it as a threat. Leaders play a pivotal role in instilling the belief that "nothing is permanent," empowering employees to remain agile and open-minded in the face of challenges. Through effective communication, support, and recognition of employee efforts, leaders cultivate a sense of purpose and motivation among their teams, driving engagement and commitment. Resilient employees demonstrate strong problem-solving skills, stress management abilities, and a willingness to learn and adapt.

They collaborate effectively, share knowledge, and support one another, fostering a culture of collaboration and teamwork. During crises or disruptions, resilient employees remain focused, resourceful, and solution-oriented, enabling the organisation to navigate challenges and maintain business continuity. Ultimately, leadership plays a crucial role in nurturing employee resilience and creating an adaptable, innovative, and high-performing workforce essential for driving organisational success in an ever-evolving business landscape.

"Nothing is permanent" OR "everything is temporary" are the phrases which must be embedded in the cultural environment which will keep the employees resilient and more open to change and better equipped to handle it. Employees belonging to such an environment respond swiftly to changing circumstances and capitalise on emerging opportunities.

Resilient individuals possess strong problem-solving skills and a proactive mindset, approaching challenges as opportunities for growth and innovation. Their ability to think creatively and generate new ideas can fuel organisational agility and foster a culture of continuous improvement.

"In the middle of difficulty lies opportunity." – *Albert Einstein*

Preparing employee resilience will help with stress management, enabling us to maintain productivity and employee well-being, avoid burnout situations, and sustain high levels of performance during demanding times.

I can do things you cannot; you can do things I cannot; together, we can do great things. - *Mother Teresa*

By promoting collaboration and teamwork, resilient employees reflect an inclination to seek support, share knowledge and collaborate with colleagues, leading to increased cohesion and synergy within teams. This collaborative spirit enhances agility by facilitating efficient communication, information sharing and collective problem-solving.

"Do not judge me by my success, judge me by how many times I fell down and got back up again." - *Nelson Mandela*

"It's kind of fun to do the impossible." - *Walt Disney*

Resilience fosters a learning and growth mindset among employees, they embrace challenges as opportunities to learn and grow and are more likely to seek out new knowledge and develop new skills. This continuous learning and growth orientation are crucial for organisations to stay ahead in a rapidly evolving business landscape.

"The greatest leader is not necessarily the one who does the greatest things. He is the one that gets the people to do the greatest things." – *Ronald Reagan, former U.S. president.*

- **Establishing a Resilient Culture:** Leaders cultivate an environment of trust and belonging, fostering employee resilience and adaptability.

- **Embracing Change:** Instilling the belief that "nothing is permanent" encourages employees to remain agile and open to change, seizing opportunities for growth.

- **Problem-Solving and Innovation:** Resilient individuals demonstrate strong problem-solving skills and a proactive mindset, driving innovation and continuous improvement.

- **Stress Management and Well-being:** Building employee resilience promotes stress management, sustaining productivity and well-being during challenging times.

- **Collaboration and Teamwork:** Resilient employees foster collaboration and teamwork, enhancing communication, synergy, and collective problem-solving.

- **Learning and Growth Mindset:** Resilience nurtures a learning and growth mindset, encouraging employees to embrace challenges as opportunities for personal and professional development.

- **Impact on Engagement and Retention:** Resilient employees feel empowered, supported, and valued, leading to higher engagement, job satisfaction, and retention rates.

- **Crisis Management and Business Continuity:** Resilience enables employees to remain focused and adaptable during crises, supporting business continuity efforts and effective problem-solving.

- **Leadership Role:** Leaders play a crucial role in nurturing employee resilience and fostering an adaptable, innovative, and collaborative workforce essential for navigating uncertain business environments.

Building employee resilience is essential for organisational success in today's dynamic and uncertain business landscape. Leaders create a culture of resilience by fostering trust, adaptability, and a proactive mindset among employees. Encouraging employees to embrace change as an opportunity for growth and innovation cultivates agility and responsiveness within the organisation. Resilient employees demonstrate strong problem-solving skills, stress management abilities, and a commitment to continuous learning and development. They collaborate effectively, support one another, and remain focused during crises, contributing to business continuity and effective problem-solving. Leadership plays a critical role in nurturing employee resilience, empowering teams to navigate challenges, seize opportunities, and drive organisational success.

Empowering Leadership Through Effective Delegation

Delegation is not merely assigning tasks; it is a strategic approach that empowers teams, develops skills, and fosters a culture of trust and accountability. Effective delegation allows leaders to distribute workload efficiently, enabling their teams to focus on core objectives and achieve organisational success. When leaders delegate responsibilities, they are not only entrusting tasks to their teams but also nurturing future leaders who will uphold the organisation's values and drive its mission forward.

Empowering employees to lead their respective areas instils a sense of ownership and accountability. These emerging leaders are motivated to surpass expectations, driven by the trust and confidence bestowed upon them. They feel empowered to explore new ideas and initiatives, adding value to their tasks and contributing to the organisation's overall objectives. Additionally, by managing the expectations of their subordinates, they learn to navigate leadership roles under the mentorship of experienced leaders, providing them with a supportive environment to innovate, focus, and demonstrate courage.

In essence, delegation serves as the cornerstone of successful leadership. It not only allows leaders to effectively manage their workload but also cultivates a culture of leadership development and innovation within the organisation. Through strategic delegation, leaders pave the way for future success by empowering their teams to excel and thrive in their respective roles.

Leadership Lessons from the Bhagavad Gita: Wisdom for Modern Leaders

Disclaimer: This section draws insights from the Bhagavad Gita solely for their universal wisdom and applicability to leadership principles, irrespective of religious affiliations.

The Bhagavad Gita, revered across cultures and religions, offers timeless wisdom and guidance for leaders seeking inspiration and insight. Beyond its religious significance, the Gita has influenced numerous thinkers and leaders throughout history, transcending boundaries of nationality and creed. Renowned figures such as Mahatma Gandhi, Aldous Huxley, and J. Robert Oppenheimer have found solace and inspiration in its teachings, drawing from its themes of selflessness, purpose, and spiritual liberation.

Leadership Lessons from the Bhagavad Gita:

- **Being A Role Model:** The Gita emphasises the importance of leading by example, demonstrating inner balance, and earning respect through courage and integrity. Leaders who embody these qualities inspire harmony and unity within their organisations.

- **Aligning Purpose and Profit:** Leaders are guided to align financial success with a higher purpose, uniting employees around shared values and goals. By fostering a seamless connection between profit and purpose, leaders create a sense of purposeful direction within their organisations.

- **Dharma In Decision-Making:** Dharma, or one's intrinsic duty, serves as a compass for ethical decision-making. Leaders are encouraged to uphold values such as fairness, justice, and integrity, aligning their actions with the greater good.

- **Managing Conflicts and Ego:** The Gita teaches leaders to develop emotional intelligence and overcome desires and attachments through self-inquiry and mindfulness. By cultivating inner balance and awareness, leaders navigate conflicts with equanimity and humility.

- **Servant Leadership:** Selfless service is central to Gita's teachings, guiding leaders to act for the greater good without attachment to outcomes. Leaders who embody servant leadership uplift individuals and society, rooted in integrity and authenticity.

- **Mindfulness And Focus:** Leaders are encouraged to turn inward, cultivating self-awareness and clarity of thought. By remaining present and focused, leaders make informed decisions and inspire confidence in their teams.

- **Adaptability To Change:** The Gita challenges perceptions of reality and impermanence, urging leaders to embrace change while anchoring themselves in inner wisdom. Leaders who navigate change with equanimity foster stability and resilience within their organisations.

- **Building Teamwork and Collaboration:** Recognising the interconnectedness of individuals, leaders galvanise teams around shared missions and purposes. By inspiring collaboration and harnessing collective potential, leaders drive organisational success.

In essence, the Bhagavad Gita offers profound insights for leaders seeking to navigate complex challenges and inspire meaningful change. By integrating these timeless teachings into their leadership approach, modern leaders can foster resilience, integrity, and purpose within their organisations.

Essential Strengths for Effective Leadership

In assuming a leadership role, a diverse set of strengths proves indispensable. Foremost among these are leadership skills, which serve as the bedrock of effective leadership. However, the multifaceted nature of leadership demands a broader spectrum of abilities, encompassing both soft skills and active listening capabilities.

Effective leadership hinges on a nuanced interplay of soft skills, each contributing to the leader's ability to inspire, guide, and empower their team. Among these crucial attributes are adept communication skills, allowing leaders to convey their vision clearly and foster meaningful connections within the team. Additionally, empathy emerges as a cornerstone of effective leadership, enabling leaders to understand and address the needs of their team members with compassion and sensitivity.

A customer-focused mindset further distinguishes exceptional leaders, as they prioritise the satisfaction and well-being of their clients or stakeholders. Moreover, trustworthiness emerges as a non-negotiable trait, underpinning the foundation of trust between leaders and their team members. By cultivating a reputation for reliability and integrity, leaders foster an environment of mutual respect and collaboration.

Creative thinking serves as a catalyst for innovation and problem-solving, allowing leaders to navigate complex challenges with ingenuity and resourcefulness. Flexibility and agility are equally indispensable, enabling leaders to adapt to evolving circumstances and seize emerging opportunities with ease.

Furthermore, selflessness and versatility characterise effective leaders, as they prioritise the collective success and well-being of their team over personal gain. This selfless approach fosters a culture of collaboration and cooperation, driving the team towards shared objectives with unity and purpose.

Lastly, a quick learning ability emerges as a key asset for leaders, empowering them to stay abreast of industry trends, technological advancements, and best practices. By continually expanding their knowledge and skill set, leaders enhance their efficacy and effectiveness in managing and motivating their teams.

In essence, the ideal strengths for a leadership position encompass a diverse array of qualities, spanning from communication and empathy to creativity and adaptability. By embodying these attributes, leaders can inspire trust, foster collaboration, and drive meaningful progress within their organisations.

Leadership skills are indispensable for fostering success and cultivating an environment of effectiveness, resilience, and positivity within a team. While competence is certainly important, strong leaders recognise that their role extends beyond mere proficiency. Instead, they aim for excellence in their leadership approach, continually seeking opportunities for growth and development.

Investing in the enhancement of leadership skills is paramount, as it serves as the catalyst for unlocking the full potential of every individual within the team. By honing their leadership abilities, leaders empower their team members to thrive, innovate, and contribute meaningfully to the collective goals of the organisation.

Moreover, the impact of effective leadership extends far beyond the confines of the workplace. As leaders refine their skills and lead by example, they become catalysts for growth and progress within their broader communities and even at the national level. By inspiring others and fostering a culture of collaboration and excellence, strong leaders drive positive change and elevate the performance and well-being of society as a whole.

In essence, the pursuit of continuous improvement in leadership skills is not only beneficial for individual leaders but also essential for the advancement and prosperity of businesses, communities, and nations alike. By prioritising the development of strong leadership capabilities, we pave the way for sustainable growth, resilience, and success in all aspects of life.

Leadership Style

Leadership encompasses a diverse array of styles, ranging from innate attributes to intentionally cultivated qualities. Some individuals possess natural talents that predispose them to leadership roles, while others actively choose to develop their leadership skills to make a positive impact on their followers. Regardless of the approach, effective leadership is characterized by the ability to inspire, motivate, and guide others toward shared goals and aspirations.

At the core of successful leadership lies the foundation of trust. Leaders who prioritize transparency, reliability, and accountability instil confidence in their followers, fostering an environment of trust and mutual respect. By consistently delivering on promises and commitments, leaders not only demonstrate their integrity but also enhance engagement and commitment among their team members. The trust garnered through consistent actions serves as a powerful catalyst for boosting morale, productivity, and overall team cohesion.

Cherished leaders distinguish themselves by leading with honesty, integrity, and respect. These qualities are not merely desirable traits but essential components of strong and enduring relationships built on a foundation of trust. By prioritizing transparency, acting with integrity, and treating others with respect, cherished leaders cultivate an environment where individuals feel valued, supported, and empowered to contribute their best efforts. As a result, strong relationships based on trust form the cornerstone of effective leadership, enabling leaders to inspire loyalty, foster collaboration, and achieve collective success.

Navigating Leadership Landscapes: Transactional vs Transformational Leadership

Transactional and transformational leadership represent contrasting approaches to leadership, each with its own set of characteristics, styles, and impacts on organizational dynamics.

Transactional leadership focuses on the exchange of resources, rewards, and punishments between leaders and followers to achieve desired outcomes. In this model, leaders establish clear expectations, set specific goals, and provide rewards or sanctions based on performance. Transactional leaders typically emphasize task completion, efficiency, and adherence to established procedures and protocols. They use contingent rewards, such as bonuses, promotions, or recognition, to motivate followers to meet objectives and fulfil their responsibilities. Additionally, transactional leaders may also employ management by exception, intervening only when deviations from established standards occur and addressing issues through corrective action.

On the other hand, transformational leadership centres on inspiring and empowering followers to transcend their self-interests and work towards collective goals that align with the organization's vision and values. Transformational leaders articulate a compelling vision for the future, challenge the status quo, and motivate followers to strive for excellence and innovation.

They exhibit charisma, enthusiasm, and passion, inspiring trust and admiration among their followers. Transformational leaders foster a sense of purpose, belonging, and intrinsic motivation, encouraging individuals to embrace change, take ownership of their work, and unleash their full potential. Moreover, transformational leaders cultivate strong relationships, provide mentorship and support, and serve as role models for ethical behaviour and personal development.

While transactional leadership focuses on achieving immediate goals through structured exchanges and contingencies, transformational leadership seeks to inspire long-term change and growth by empowering and mobilizing followers. Transactional leadership is effective in maintaining stability, ensuring compliance, and achieving short-term objectives, whereas transformational leadership is instrumental in fostering innovation, adaptability, and organizational learning. Ultimately, the most effective leaders often employ a combination of transactional and transformational approaches, adapting their leadership style to the needs and challenges of different situations and contexts.

Driving Results: The Leadership of Execution

Leaders with an execution domain are the driving force behind turning ideas into tangible results. They possess a unique set of qualities and characteristics that enable them to bring plans to fruition and achieve organizational goals effectively. One key trait of leaders in this domain is their unwavering determination and focus on execution. They are relentless in their pursuit of objectives and demonstrate a strong sense of commitment to seeing tasks through to completion.

These leaders exhibit the qualities of achievers, constantly striving for excellence and pushing themselves and their teams to reach new heights. They maintain a high level of consistency in their actions and decisions, ensuring that progress is made steadily and reliably over time. Their ability to stay focused amidst distractions enables them to stay on track and overcome obstacles that may arise along the way.

In addition, leaders with an execution domain possess strong organizational skills, such as being arrangers who can efficiently manage resources and coordinate efforts to achieve desired outcomes. They approach tasks with a deliberate mindset, carefully planning each step and considering potential risks and challenges. Their sense of responsibility drives them to take ownership of tasks and outcomes, inspiring confidence and trust in their leadership.

Moreover, these leaders often hold strong beliefs in their vision and goals, motivating themselves and others to work with dedication and passion. They demonstrate discipline in their approach to work, adhering to deadlines and standards with a sense of professionalism and integrity. Furthermore, their ability to address setbacks and challenges with a restorative mindset allows them to learn from failures and adapt their strategies for future success.

Overall, leaders with an execution domain play a crucial role in driving progress and achieving results within organizations. Their combination of determination, focus, and organizational skills enables them to effectively implement solutions and turn vision into reality.

Mastering Influence: Leadership in the Domain of Persuasion

Leaders with influence domains possess a unique ability to sway opinions, mobilize resources, and garner support for their team's initiatives both within and outside the organization. They excel at articulating the team's vision, values, and goals in a compelling manner that resonates with diverse stakeholders. These leaders are adept at networking, building alliances, and leveraging their interpersonal skills to cultivate relationships with key decision-makers and influencers. They possess qualities such as being activators, driven by competition, and seeking significance in their endeavours. With a commanding presence and persuasive communication style, they can effectively rally support for their team's initiatives and drive consensus among stakeholders. Additionally, these leaders exhibit self-assurance and confidence in their abilities, inspiring trust and loyalty among their followers. Overall, leaders with influence domains play a pivotal role in amplifying their team's impact and extending their reach to a broader audience, thereby contributing to the organization's success and growth.

Nurturing Unity: Leadership in Relationship Building Domain

Leadership within the relationship-building domain emphasizes the cultivation of strong interpersonal connections and the creation of a cohesive team environment. Leaders in this domain excel at fostering positive and harmonious relationships among team members, serving as the glue that binds the group together. Their leadership style minimizes distractions and maintains the collective energy of the team at a high and engaged level.

These leaders emerge as mentors who not only provide guidance but also inspire and push others towards bigger and better achievements. They prioritize empathy, understanding the unique needs and perspectives of each team member, and adapt their approach accordingly. By recognizing and valuing individual differences, they create an inclusive environment where everyone feels respected and valued.

Positivity is a hallmark of leadership within the relationship-building domain. These leaders cultivate an optimistic outlook and encourage optimism among team members, even in the face of challenges or setbacks. They leverage their strong communication skills to foster open dialogue, promote collaboration, and resolve conflicts constructively.

Furthermore, leaders in this domain possess a deep sense of connectedness and invest time and effort in building meaningful relationships with team members. They prioritize the development of trust and rapport, creating a safe space where individuals feel comfortable expressing themselves and sharing ideas.

Ultimately, leaders in the relationship-building domain are relators who excel at building bridges between team members, fostering a sense of belonging, and creating a supportive and inclusive team culture.

Guiding Visionaries: Leadership in Strategic Thinking Domain

Leadership within the strategic thinking domain is characterized by a steadfast focus on the future and a commitment to guiding teams towards long-term success. These leaders play a crucial role in keeping the team aligned with organizational goals and objectives, leveraging their ability to absorb, analyse, and interpret information to make informed decisions and drive strategic initiatives.

At the core of their leadership style is a dedication to continuous learning and growth. Leaders in this domain are constantly seeking new insights and perspectives, challenging the status quo, and pushing the boundaries of conventional thinking. They possess a keen analytical mind, capable of dissecting complex problems and identifying underlying patterns and trends.

One of the key strengths of leaders with strategic thinking is their ability to connect past events with present circumstances and anticipate future possibilities. They excel at synthesizing information from various sources, providing valuable context and insights that inform decision-making and shape strategic direction.

Furthermore, leaders in this domain are adept at exploring countless possibilities for growth and innovation. They encourage their teams to think creatively and critically, challenging them to explore new ideas and approaches that can drive organizational success. By fostering a culture of innovation and experimentation, these leaders inspire their teams to push beyond the status quo and embrace change as a catalyst for growth.

Strategic thinkers also possess a futuristic mindset, envisioning potential scenarios and outcomes and developing strategic plans to navigate them effectively. They excel at articulating a compelling vision for the future and rallying their teams around shared goals and objectives.

Ultimately, leaders in the strategic thinking domain possess a unique blend of analytical prowess, visionary insight, and strategic acumen. They serve as catalysts for innovation and change, driving organizational growth and success through their ability to anticipate opportunities and navigate challenges with clarity and foresight.

Compassionate Leadership: Fostering Trust and Empowerment

Leadership characterized by compassion is a powerful force that drives positive change within organizations. These leaders approach their role with a deep sense of empathy, understanding, and care for the people they lead. They prioritize the well-being and development of their team members, fostering a supportive and nurturing work environment where individuals feel valued, respected, and empowered.

At the heart of compassionate leadership is the ability to connect with others on a personal level, much like one would with friends and family members. These leaders demonstrate genuine concern for the welfare of their team members, taking the time to listen to their concerns, acknowledge their contributions, and provide support when needed. By building strong relationships based on trust, respect, and authenticity, compassionate leaders create a sense of belonging and camaraderie within the team.

One of the key strengths of compassionate leaders is their ability to inspire loyalty, engagement, and productivity among their team members. By demonstrating care and understanding, these leaders instil a sense of purpose and motivation in their team, encouraging individuals to go above and beyond in pursuit of shared goals and objectives. Moreover, compassionate leaders create an environment where team members feel safe to take risks, share ideas, and express themselves freely, leading to increased innovation, collaboration, and problem-solving.

Compassionate leaders also play a vital role in supporting the personal and professional growth of their team members. They provide mentorship, guidance, and encouragement, helping individuals unlock their full potential and overcome challenges. By investing in the development and well-being of their team, compassionate leaders foster a culture of continuous learning, growth, and resilience.

Furthermore, compassionate leadership has a ripple effect that extends beyond the immediate team to the broader organization. These leaders set the tone for organizational culture, promoting values such as empathy, kindness, and inclusivity. As a result, employees feel more connected to the organization's mission and values, leading to higher levels of satisfaction, retention, and overall performance.

In summary, compassionate leadership is a transformative force that cultivates trust, empowerment, and belonging within organizations. By prioritizing the well-being of their team members and fostering a supportive and nurturing environment, compassionate leaders drive positive outcomes, create a culture of excellence, and, ultimately, propel the organization towards success and fulfilment.

Leading with Stability and Inspiring Hope: Navigating Through Uncertainty

Leadership characterized by stability and hope is a beacon of strength and reassurance in times of turbulence and change. These leaders possess steadfast core values and unwavering principles that serve as a guiding light for their team members. By fostering an environment of security, support, and peace, they instil confidence, resilience, and optimism in the face of adversity.

At the heart of leadership with stability and hope is the ability to provide a sense of security and strength to followers. These leaders demonstrate consistency, reliability, and dependability in their words and actions, serving as a stabilizing force amidst chaos and uncertainty. By upholding core values and principles, they create a foundation of trust and confidence that empowers individuals to navigate challenges with resilience and determination.

Moreover, leaders with stability and hope serve as pillars of support for their team members, offering guidance, encouragement, and reassurance during times of crises, growth, and change. Their messages and actions convey strength and resilience, inspiring confidence and faith in the face of uncertainty. By modelling calmness, composure, and grace under pressure, these leaders instil a sense of hope and optimism that energizes and uplifts their team members.

Stability and hope are not only essential for individual well-being but also play a crucial role in decision-making and navigating organizational directions. Leaders with stable core values make decisions with integrity, clarity, and foresight, guided by a deep sense of purpose and conviction. Their unwavering commitment to their values inspires trust and confidence in their leadership, fostering cohesion and unity within the organization.

Furthermore, hope serves as a powerful catalyst for growth, transformation, and renewal. Leaders who infuse their vision with hope inspire individuals to see beyond the present challenges and envision a brighter future. By nurturing a sense of hopefulness and optimism, these leaders ignite passion, creativity, and innovation, driving positive change and progress.

In summary, leadership with stability and hope is instrumental in guiding individuals and organizations through times of uncertainty and change. By embodying steadfast core values, providing support and reassurance, and inspiring hope for the future, these leaders create a culture of resilience, optimism, and possibility. Through their unwavering leadership, they empower individuals to overcome obstacles, seize opportunities, and achieve collective success.

The Power of Charismatic Leadership: Inspiring Others with Genuine Care and Confidence

Charismatic leadership transcends mere charm or magnetism; it embodies a genuine concern for others and a deep sense of authenticity and confidence. It is a reflection of true character and a sincere desire to uplift and empower those around you. As Michelle Obama aptly stated, charismatic leaders genuinely seek to understand and uplift others, making them feel valued and important.

At the core of charismatic leadership is the ability to inspire and influence others through personal charm and persuasive communication. Charismatic leaders serve as role models, captivating their followers with their compelling vision and infectious enthusiasm. They possess strong communication skills, using language effectively to inspire action and motivate others to reach their full potential.

In essence, charismatic leaders are adept at charging others with positive energy and leveraging their skills and abilities to achieve collective goals. They inspire young people to become leaders themselves and actively contribute to the development of others. By leading by example and displaying unwavering confidence and a can-do attitude, charismatic leaders empower others to believe in themselves and their capabilities.

Charismatic leaders communicate with purpose and passion, using their tone of voice, language, gestures, and facial expressions to connect with their followers on an emotional level. They exude high energy and enthusiasm, captivating attention and inspiring action through their infectious zeal and unwavering conviction.

In conclusion, charismatic leadership is a powerful force for inspiring and motivating others to reach new heights of achievement. By genuinely caring for others, communicating with purpose and passion, and leading by example with confidence and enthusiasm, charismatic leaders create a culture of empowerment, engagement, and excellence. Through their inspirational leadership, they leave a lasting impact on those they lead, igniting a spark of possibility and potential in every individual they encounter.

The Transformative Power of Empathetic Leadership

Empathetic leadership transcends manipulation and control, instead focusing on genuine understanding and collaboration with employees to achieve shared goals and objectives. This authentic approach fosters credibility and trust, laying the foundation for a positive work environment where performance and results flourish.

Empathetic leadership yields numerous benefits, driving performance and productivity while enhancing overall well-being within the organization. By prioritizing empathy, leaders cultivate engagement, collaboration, and innovation among their teams, resulting in tangible improvements across various facets of the business.

Employee Engagement: Through active listening and genuine care, empathetic leaders create an environment where employees feel valued and understood, driving higher levels of engagement and motivation to contribute their best efforts.

Communication and Collaboration: Empathetic leaders foster open communication and encourage diverse perspectives, promoting trust and collaboration among team members. This inclusive approach stimulates creativity and innovation, leading to more effective problem-solving.

Morale and Well-being: By recognizing and supporting their team members' needs, empathetic leaders boost morale and create a positive work culture that prioritizes employee well-being. This leads to reduced stress and burnout, contributing to a healthier and happier workforce.

Problem-solving and Innovation: Empathetic leaders embrace diversity and inclusion, leveraging the unique insights of each team member to drive innovation and creativity. By valuing different perspectives, they foster an environment where novel ideas can flourish.

Loyalty and Retention: Through mentorship and support, empathetic leaders cultivate loyalty and commitment among their team members, reducing turnover and retaining top talent within the organization.

Customer Satisfaction: Empathetic leadership extends beyond internal interactions to shape customer service practices, resulting in higher levels of customer satisfaction, loyalty, and business success.

Furthermore, empathetic leadership bridges generation gaps and cultural differences, enhancing leaders' ability to connect with individuals from diverse backgrounds and personalities. This heightened empathy fosters stronger relationships and trust, ultimately empowering individuals and teams to surpass expectations and deliver exceptional results.

In summary, empathetic leadership creates a ripple effect throughout the organization, driving positive outcomes that extend beyond performance metrics to encompass employee well-being, customer satisfaction, and overall business success. By prioritizing empathy, understanding, and support, leaders can inspire their teams to achieve greatness and thrive in today's dynamic business landscape.

The Impact of Collaborative Leadership on Organizational Success

Collaborative leadership embodies a balanced and inclusive approach that fosters public value and drives impactful outcomes across various teams and departments within an organization. By promoting a culture of shared vision, collective influence, and mutual respect, collaborative leaders empower their teams to thrive and excel.

Collaborative leaders possess a unique ability to listen attentively to diverse perspectives, take calculated risks, and remain optimistic about the future. They actively involve others in decision-making processes, share power and knowledge generously, and recognize and celebrate collective achievements. This collaborative ethos permeates throughout the organization, creating a culture of idea-sharing, shared leadership, and mutual recognition.

The ripple effects of collaborative leadership extend beyond the leader-team dynamic, influencing the broader organizational culture and performance. Employees in collaborative environments feel valued, motivated, and engaged, leading to heightened morale and productivity. This positive work environment fosters innovation, creativity, and problem-solving, driving improved business performance and outcomes.

Collaborative leadership aligns with the intrinsic drivers of motivation: purpose, mastery, and autonomy. By articulating a compelling purpose, providing autonomy in roles, and fostering opportunities for skill development and mastery, collaborative leaders inspire their teams to perform at their best. This sense of purpose and autonomy instils a greater sense of ownership and commitment among employees, leading to increased job satisfaction and retention.

Ultimately, collaborative leadership not only drives organizational success but also creates a fulfilling and empowering work environment where individuals are motivated to contribute their best efforts towards shared goals. By embracing collaboration, sharing credit, and nurturing a culture of mutual respect and trust, leaders can unlock the full potential of their teams and pave the way for sustained success and growth.

Navigating the Divide: Strategic Leadership vs. Operational Leadership

Strategic leaders and operational leaders play distinct yet complementary roles in steering organizations towards success. While both are crucial for achieving organizational objectives, they operate at different levels and focus on different aspects of leadership.

A strategic leader is a visionary architect who sets the course for the organization's future. They possess a forward-thinking mindset, constantly scanning the horizon for emerging opportunities and threats. Strategic leaders think strategically, analysing market trends, competitive landscapes, and internal capabilities to formulate long-term plans and goals. They inspire and mobilize others to rally behind their vision, leveraging their charisma and persuasive abilities to garner support. While strategic leaders may delegate day-to-day operational tasks, they remain actively involved in shaping the organization's strategic direction and ensuring alignment with its overarching mission and values. Their authority emanates from their strategic acumen and ability to articulate a compelling vision for the future.

In contrast, an operational leader is the hands-on executor responsible for translating strategic plans into tangible actions and results. They oversee the day-to-day operations of the organization, ensuring that processes run smoothly, resources are allocated efficiently, and objectives are met. Operational leaders work closely with cross-functional teams to implement strategies, streamline workflows, and optimize performance. They possess strong managerial skills, adept at budgeting, decision-making, and problem-solving. Operational leaders excel in analysing data, identifying operational inefficiencies, and making real-time adjustments to improve productivity and efficiency. While they may lack the visionary outlook of strategic leaders, their pragmatic approach and attention to detail are essential for executing strategic initiatives and driving organizational success.

In summary, strategic leaders set the direction and vision for the organization, while operational leaders focus on executing plans and achieving tangible results. Both types of leadership are essential for navigating the complex challenges of today's business environment, and successful organizations often rely on a symbiotic relationship between strategic and operational leadership to thrive and prosper.

Leadership Strengths and Challenges

Leadership is a multifaceted journey filled with opportunities for growth, impact, and fulfilment, but it also presents its fair share of challenges and complexities. Effective leadership requires a unique blend of strengths and abilities, as well as the resilience to overcome obstacles and adapt to changing circumstances.

Strengths of Leadership: Great leadership transcends appearance, focusing instead on unlocking the potential within individuals and organizations. It encompasses the ability to execute plans, influence others, build relationships, and engage in strategic thinking. True leaders inspire and empower others, leaving a lasting impact on people's lives. Leadership can emerge at any age and in any role, influencing individuals or entire organizations across various sectors of society.

Leadership qualities include empathy, creativity, discipline, strategic thinking, humility, decisiveness, and effective communication. Authentic leaders stay true to themselves and surround themselves with individuals who complement their strengths, fostering a network of strong leaders who continue to grow and evolve over time.

As Mervyn Davies, Chairman of Standard, emphasizes, the true impact of leadership extends far beyond the present moment, shaping the trajectory of organizations long after the leader has moved on.

Challenges of Leadership: In today's rapidly evolving business landscape, leaders face a myriad of challenges that require adaptability, foresight, and resilience. These challenges include:

- **Technological Advancements:** While technology offers numerous benefits, such as increased efficiency and speed, it also presents challenges related to data security and privacy. Leaders must navigate the complexities of technological innovation while ensuring alignment with business objectives.

- **Remote Work Dynamics:** The rise of remote work poses challenges in fostering team cohesion, motivation, and productivity. Leaders must find innovative ways to support and engage remote teams while maintaining organizational culture.

- **Talent Management:** Attracting, retaining, and developing top talent, especially among the younger generation, poses significant challenges. Leaders must create environments that foster high engagement and professional growth to meet evolving workforce expectations.

- **Environmental and Social Responsibility:** Leaders are increasingly accountable for sustainability and corporate responsibility, balancing strategic objectives with environmental and social impact considerations.

- **Global Expansion:** Expanding into international markets requires leaders to navigate diverse cultures, regulations, and market dynamics. Geopolitical developments and changing trade regulations further complicate global business operations.

Overcoming these challenges requires leaders to demonstrate adaptability, resilience, empathy, and a commitment to continuous learning. Seeking external expertise and fostering collaboration are also crucial strategies for addressing complex issues in today's dynamic business environment.

In summary, effective leadership is characterized by a diverse set of strengths, including innovation, integrity, active listening, honesty, visionary thinking, and problem-solving abilities. By embracing these qualities and navigating challenges with resilience and agility, leaders can inspire positive change and drive organizational success in an ever-changing world.

Navigating Resistance to Change: Strategies for Effective Leadership

Resistance to change is a natural response that often arises when individuals perceive a shift in the status quo as a threat to their comfort, stability, or familiarity. As leaders navigate organizational transformations or initiatives, they must anticipate and manage resistance effectively to ensure successful implementation and adoption.

Addressing Resistance: Leaders play a critical role in addressing resistance to change by providing support, guidance, and reassurance to team members who may be hesitant or apprehensive about embracing new ways of working. This involves acknowledging and validating individuals' concerns and fears while also helping them understand the rationale behind the proposed changes and the potential benefits they offer.

Understanding the Root Causes: Resistance to change can stem from various sources, including fear of the unknown, loss of control, perceived lack of competence, or scepticism about the benefits of change. Leaders must take the time to identify and address these underlying concerns through open dialogue, active listening, and empathy.

Effective Strategies for Managing Resistance:

- **Education and Communication:** Leaders can mitigate resistance by transparently communicating the reasons for change, the expected outcomes, and the potential impact on individuals and the organization. This communication can take various forms, including one-on-one discussions, group meetings, and written communications such as memos or reports.

- **Participation and Involvement:** Involving team members in the change process can foster a sense of ownership and commitment. Leaders can create opportunities for participation through special committees, task forces, or focus groups, where employees can provide input, share concerns, and collaborate on solutions.

- **Facilitation and Support:** Providing emotional support and offering training and resources can help individuals navigate the challenges associated with change. Leaders can organize instructional meetings, coaching sessions, or counselling services to equip employees with the skills and knowledge needed to adapt to new circumstances.

- **Open Communication Channels:** Establishing open and transparent communication channels is essential for building trust and fostering a collaborative environment. Leaders should encourage dialogue, listen to feedback, and address concerns in a timely and empathetic manner. By creating a culture of open communication, leaders can cultivate a sense of psychological safety where team members feel comfortable expressing their thoughts and concerns.

In essence, managing resistance to change requires a multifaceted approach that combines education, participation, facilitation, and open communication. By acknowledging individuals' concerns, involving them in the change process, and providing support and guidance, leaders can effectively navigate resistance and facilitate successful organizational transitions.

Overcoming Communication Challenges in Leadership

Inadequate communication poses a persistent challenge for leaders across various organizational levels. Whether interacting with clients, team members, fellow leaders, or senior management, leaders often grapple with communication breakdowns that can impede productivity and hinder goal achievement. Effective leadership hinges on robust communication skills, as leaders must navigate complex interpersonal dynamics, convey strategic objectives, and foster a culture of transparency and collaboration.

Transparency lies at the heart of effective communication within a workplace. When leaders ensure that each team member's goals, responsibilities, and expectations align with the overarching goals and objectives of the company, they foster a sense of clarity and purpose among their teams. This alignment not only enhances accountability but also cultivates a shared sense of mission, driving collective effort towards organizational success.

Establishing an open communication platform and holding regular meetings are essential strategies for promoting engagement, unity, and cohesiveness within teams. By providing a forum for dialogue and feedback, leaders create opportunities for team members to voice their concerns, share ideas, and contribute to decision-making processes. Moreover, such platforms foster a culture of inclusivity and mutual respect, where every voice is valued and heard.

In instances of disputes or conflicts, effective leadership intervention is crucial for resolving issues and restoring harmony within teams. Leaders play a pivotal role in facilitating constructive dialogue, mediating disagreements, and guiding team members towards mutually beneficial solutions. By demonstrating empathy, fairness, and impartiality, leaders can build trust and foster a collaborative environment conducive to conflict resolution.

Active listening is a fundamental skill that leaders must cultivate to enhance communication effectiveness. By attentively listening to the perspectives, concerns, and feedback of team members, leaders demonstrate respect and empathy, fostering a culture of open communication and trust. Moreover, active listening enables leaders to gain valuable insights, identify underlying issues, and make informed decisions that resonate with the needs and aspirations of their teams.

In summary, addressing the challenge of inadequate communication requires leaders to prioritize transparency, establish open channels of communication, intervene effectively in disputes, and hone their active listening skills. By embracing these principles, leaders can foster a culture of collaboration, engagement, and mutual respect, driving organizational success and enhancing team performance.

Navigating Stakeholder Alignment: Overcoming Challenges for Organizational Success

Lack of alignment among stakeholders presents a significant challenge for organizations, as it can lead to confusion, inefficiency, and, ultimately, poor outcomes. Alignment with stakeholders regarding expectations and priorities is paramount, as it establishes a common understanding and direction for the work environment, ensuring that efforts are focused and coordinated towards shared objectives.

When stakeholders are not aligned, challenges arise that can hinder productivity and impact the quality of deliverables. For instance, misalignment may manifest when an employee agrees on a set of priorities with a key stakeholder, and the team executes tasks accordingly, delivering the final product on time. However, despite meeting agreed-upon criteria, the delivered solution may not align with the actual needs or expectations of the stakeholders.

In such scenarios, confusion ensues among the delivery team, as they fulfilled their obligations based on the agreed-upon requirements. However, the discrepancy arises from a lack of alignment among stakeholders themselves. This misalignment may occur horizontally, where stakeholders at the same level within the organization hold differing perspectives or priorities. Alternatively, it could stem from vertical misalignment, with discrepancies between managers and their superiors regarding overarching objectives or strategic direction.

Consequently, the organization may suffer reputational damage, as stakeholders perceive the delivered solution as inadequate or misaligned with their needs. Moreover, the wasted time and resources invested in delivering the wrong outcome can undermine trust and collaboration within the organization, impeding future efforts.

To address the challenge of stakeholder misalignment, organizations must prioritize communication, collaboration, and alignment across all levels of the organization. Clear channels of communication should be established to facilitate ongoing dialogue and ensure that expectations and priorities are consistently communicated and understood. Additionally, efforts should be made to foster a culture of transparency and accountability, where stakeholders actively engage in discussions to align their objectives and perspectives.

Furthermore, leaders play a crucial role in driving alignment by facilitating discussions, resolving conflicts, and establishing mechanisms for decision-making and prioritization. By promoting a shared understanding of goals and objectives, leaders can mitigate the risks associated with stakeholder misalignment and ensure that efforts are directed towards achieving collective success.

Navigating Long-Term Focus: Strategies for Overcoming Distractions

In today's fast-paced world, staying focused on long-term goals can be challenging due to the myriad distractions that surround us. The constant influx of information, technological advancements, and competing priorities make it difficult to maintain a clear focus on our objectives.

To combat this challenge, it's essential to implement strategies that help minimize distractions and keep our attention directed towards our long-term goals. One approach is to keep visual reminders prominently displayed in our work environment. These reminders serve as constant cues, reinforcing our commitment to our objectives and helping us stay on track.

Additionally, delegation and regular one-on-one meetings can provide valuable feedback and support, ensuring alignment with long-term goals. Dashboard analysis tools offer a comprehensive overview of performance metrics, allowing us to monitor progress and make necessary adjustments to stay aligned with our objectives.

Creating an environment that fosters goal alignment is crucial for maintaining focus. This involves establishing clear expectations, providing resources and support, and fostering a culture that values goal attainment. Surrounding oneself with supportive individuals and accountability buddies can also help reinforce commitment and provide encouragement along the way.

Breaking down long-term goals into smaller, manageable milestones can make them more achievable and provide a sense of progress. Setting up incentives for reaching these milestones can further motivate individuals and teams to stay focused and committed to their objectives.

In summary, while distractions are inevitable, implementing these strategies can help individuals and organizations maintain focus on their long-term goals amidst the complexities of the modern world. By creating a supportive environment, leveraging visual cues, and establishing clear milestones, individuals can enhance their ability to stay focused and achieve success in the long run.

Cultivating Passion: The Key to Success in Work and Beyond

Passion for one's work is not merely an abstract concept; it's a driving force that propels individuals towards success and fulfilment. When individuals are genuinely passionate about their work or projects, they are more likely to understand the needs of others and possess the determination needed to overcome obstacles and achieve success.

However, when passion is lacking, it can have detrimental effects, both on individuals and the organization. Without passion, work can become mundane, uninspired, and devoid of innovation. This lack of enthusiasm can manifest in decreased productivity, disengagement, and ultimately, hindered progress towards organizational goals.

To address this challenge, leaders can play a crucial role in fostering and nurturing passion among their team members. One effective approach is to provide constructive feedback that encourages personal and professional growth. By recognizing and acknowledging individuals' efforts and contributions, leaders can inspire passion and commitment, motivating team members to strive for excellence in their work.

Moreover, leaders can create an environment that cultivates passion by fostering a culture of openness, creativity, and collaboration. Encouraging autonomy, allowing individuals to pursue projects aligned with their interests, and providing opportunities for skill development can reignite passion and enthusiasm for work.

Ultimately, by prioritizing and nurturing passion within the workplace, leaders can unlock the full potential of their teams, driving innovation, productivity, and success. Passionate individuals are not only more engaged and fulfilled in their roles but also contribute significantly to the overall growth and success of the organization.

Mastering Clarity: The Foundation of Effective Leadership Communication

Effective leadership hinges on the ability to maintain clear communication channels. In any leadership role, whether navigating strengths or weaknesses, fostering transparent communication with team members is paramount for collective success. Leadership skills must continually evolve to align with the dynamic work environment, encompassing traits like clear communication, motivation, negotiation, and planning.

Clear communication serves as the linchpin for ensuring shared understanding and cohesion within a team. It not only keeps projects on course but also bolsters motivation and productivity among team members. By articulating objectives and expectations clearly, leaders empower individuals to thrive and contribute effectively to organizational goals. In essence, mastering clear communication nurtures an environment conducive to growth, collaboration, and achievement.

Embracing Growth: The Role of Mistakes in Leadership

Leaders, like anyone else, are fallible and can make mistakes. However, effective leaders distinguish themselves not by avoiding mistakes altogether, but by their response to them. It is crucial for leaders to recognize when errors occur, accept accountability, and take prompt corrective action or seek necessary training.

Beyond mere error avoidance, effective leaders demonstrate resilience and problem-solving prowess. They proactively identify and address challenges before they escalate, finding innovative solutions to navigate obstacles. Recognizing areas for improvement within one's leadership style is the first step toward growth. Leaders must then develop strategies to transform weaknesses into strengths, leveraging feedback and learning opportunities to refine their approach.

A learning mindset is essential for leadership development at all levels. Leaders benefit from studying both the successes and missteps of others, analysing different approaches, and adapting techniques to suit their own context. By actively seeking constructive feedback and incorporating it into their leadership approach, leaders demonstrate humility and a commitment to growth. Ultimately, it is through embracing mistakes as learning opportunities and continually refining their skills that leaders cultivate resilience and effectiveness in their roles.

Embracing Leadership Imperfections: Navigating Weaknesses with Grace

As a leader, it's essential to acknowledge that weaknesses and challenges are part of the journey, not something to be ashamed of. Instead of succumbing to frustration or despair, leaders should view these moments as opportunities for growth and improvement.

The first step in addressing leadership weaknesses is self-awareness. Leaders must recognize areas where they fall short and be open to feedback from others. Rather than dwelling on mistakes, they should focus on understanding what went wrong and devising strategies for improvement.

Seeking advice and support from various sources, including family, friends, colleagues, and subordinates, can provide valuable insights and perspectives. Delegation and mentorship are effective strategies for freeing up time and energy to work on developing skills that may be holding leaders back.

It's important for leaders to understand that they don't need to have all the answers. Humility and a willingness to seek help or consult with others when needed are traits of effective leadership. By balancing ambition with humility, embracing calculated risks, and remaining open to new ideas and approaches, leaders can continue to evolve and excel in their roles. Ultimately, it's the willingness to learn from mistakes and adapt that sets successful leaders apart.

Navigating Leadership Weaknesses: Strategies for Growth and Improvement

Recognizing and addressing leadership weaknesses is crucial for personal and organizational growth. Here are some common weaknesses and strategies for overcoming them:

- **People-Pleasing Tendencies:** Leaders who prioritize being liked may struggle with decision-making and delegation. To overcome this, seek honest feedback from employees and create a culture where open communication is encouraged. Focus on finding the balance between being approachable and assertive in your leadership style.

- **Lack of Emotional Intelligence:** Difficulty in understanding and managing emotions can hinder effective leadership. Invest in resources to enhance emotional intelligence, such as books or training programs. Practice empathy and active listening to better connect with team members and foster a supportive work environment.

- **Inability to Delegate:** Trust issues may lead to micromanagement and delayed deliverables. Work on building trust with your team by empowering them to take ownership of tasks and projects. Set clear expectations and provide guidance and support as needed, but avoid the temptation to intervene excessively.

- **Tendency to Blame Others:** Constantly blaming others can erode trust and morale within the team. Take responsibility for mistakes and use them as opportunities for learning and growth. Cultivate a culture of accountability where everyone takes ownership of their actions and works together to find solutions.

- **Failure to Listen:** Ignoring input from team members can lead to disengagement and reduced productivity. Practice active listening and show genuine interest in others' perspectives. Create opportunities for open dialogue and collaboration and ensure that everyone feels valued and heard.

By acknowledging and addressing these weaknesses, leaders can cultivate a more effective and supportive leadership style, leading to improved team dynamics and organizational success.

Maximizing Leadership Strengths: Strategies for Growth and Improvement

Understanding and leveraging your leadership strengths is essential for personal and organizational success. Here are some strategies to help you identify and capitalize on your strengths while addressing weaknesses:

- **Seek Feedback:** Ask colleagues, subordinates, and mentors for feedback on your leadership style. Their insights can provide valuable perspective on your strengths and areas for improvement. Be open to constructive criticism and use it to inform your development efforts.

- **Self-Assessment:** Regularly assess your strengths and weaknesses as a leader. Reflect on past experiences and identify patterns of success and areas where you may need to improve. Consider using assessment tools or seeking professional coaching to gain further insight into your leadership abilities.

- **Skill Development:** Focus on sharpening your top leadership skills to enhance your effectiveness. Invest time and resources in training, workshops, or courses that align with your development goals. Practice self-discipline and consistency in honing your skills to maximize your potential as a leader.

- **Goal Alignment:** Ensure that your leadership strengths align with the goals and objectives of your team and organization. Identify areas where your strengths can contribute to achieving strategic objectives and prioritize efforts accordingly. This alignment will increase your impact as a leader and drive success for your team.

- **Address Weaknesses:** Acknowledge and address any weaknesses or areas for improvement in your leadership style. Develop action plans to overcome challenges and enhance your capabilities. Seek support from mentors, colleagues, or professional development resources to assist you in addressing these areas effectively.

- **Continuous Improvement:** View leadership development as an ongoing process of growth and learning. Stay curious and proactive in seeking opportunities for improvement. Embrace feedback, experimentation, and reflection as essential components of your leadership journey.

By embracing your strengths, addressing weaknesses, and committing to continuous improvement, you can maximize your effectiveness as a leader and drive positive outcomes for yourself and your team.

Leadership Biases

Unconscious biases are deeply ingrained in human cognition and can significantly influence decision-making processes, behaviours, and interactions. These biases manifest as unintentional favouritisms, preconceptions, prejudices, and stereotypes that shape how individuals perceive and respond to others. In a leadership context, these biases can have profound implications for organizational dynamics and outcomes.

Leadership bias occurs when leaders exhibit preferences or prejudices towards certain individuals, groups, or ideas, whether consciously or unconsciously. These biases can manifest in various forms, such as favouring employees who share similar backgrounds or characteristics, overlooking diverse perspectives, or making decisions based on stereotypes rather than objective criteria.

The impact of leadership bias on an organization can be far-reaching. Biased decision-making can lead to unfair treatment, inequality, and lack of diversity and inclusion within the workforce. It can also undermine employee morale, trust, and engagement, eroding the organizational culture and hindering collaboration and innovation.

To mitigate the impact of leadership bias, leaders must first recognize and acknowledge their own biases. This requires self-awareness, introspection, and a willingness to confront uncomfortable truths about one's own attitudes and behaviours.

Leaders should actively seek feedback from others, including peers, subordinates, and mentors, to gain perspective on how their biases may be influencing their decisions and interactions.

Additionally, leaders can implement strategies to counteract bias in their decision-making processes. This may include adopting structured decision-making frameworks that prioritize objective criteria over subjective judgments, implementing diversity and inclusion initiatives to promote equitable treatment and representation, and providing bias awareness training for leaders and employees.

Creating a culture of accountability and transparency is also essential for addressing leadership bias effectively. Leaders should openly acknowledge and address instances of bias within the organization, encourage open dialogue and feedback, and hold themselves and others accountable for fair and equitable treatment.

By actively challenging and mitigating leadership bias, organizations can foster a more inclusive, equitable, and effective leadership culture that values diversity, promotes fairness, and maximizes the potential of all individuals and groups within the workforce.

Understanding Common Types of Bias in Decision-Making

Biases are inherent in human cognition and can significantly influence decision-making processes. Here are explanations of several common types of biases:

- **Actor-observer bias:** This bias refers to differences in how individuals perceive their own behaviour versus how they perceive the behaviour of others. People tend to attribute their own actions to external factors but attribute others' actions to their internal traits.

- **Anchoring bias:** This bias occurs when individuals rely heavily on the first piece of information they receive when making decisions, often leading to underestimation or overestimation of subsequent information.

- **Attentional bias:** This bias occurs when individuals focus solely on specific information while ignoring other relevant information, potentially leading to incomplete or biased judgments.

- **Availability heuristic:** This bias involves relying on immediate information that is readily available in the mind when making judgments or decisions, often leading to overestimation of the likelihood of events.

- **Confirmation bias:** This bias involves seeking out and favouring information that confirms one's existing beliefs or hypotheses while disregarding contradictory evidence.

- **Dunning-Kruger effect:** This bias refers to the tendency for individuals to overestimate their own abilities or intelligence, often leading to a lack of awareness of their own incompetence.

- **False consensus effect:** This bias involves overestimating the extent to which others agree with one's own opinions or behaviours, leading to a skewed perception of consensus.

- **Functional fixedness:** This bias occurs when individuals are unable to see objects or concepts beyond their typical functions or uses, limiting creative problem-solving and innovation.

- **Halo effect:** This bias occurs when individuals form an overall positive impression of a person, product, or brand based on specific positive qualities or characteristics.

- **Misinformation effect:** This bias occurs when the memory of an event becomes distorted or less accurate due to exposure to misinformation or post-event information.

- **Optimism bias:** This bias involves overestimating the likelihood of positive outcomes and underestimating the likelihood of negative outcomes, leading to unrealistic optimism.

- **Self-serving bias:** This bias involves attributing success to internal factors while attributing failure to external factors, protecting one's self-esteem and self-image.

Awareness of these biases is crucial for effective decision-making and can help individuals mitigate their impact by employing strategies such as critical thinking, seeking diverse perspectives, and challenging assumptions.

Understanding Cognitive Bias: Its Impact and Influences

Cognitive bias is a prevalent phenomenon characterized by unconscious, automatic errors in thinking that occur when information is misinterpreted, leading to deviations from rational judgment. Here's an elaboration on cognitive bias, its impact, and influencing factors:

- **Definition:** Cognitive bias refers to repeated and systematic errors of thought that result from mental shortcuts or patterns of thinking. These biases can influence our understanding, assessment of situations, interpretation of information, and decision-making processes, often leading to deviations from rational and objective thinking.

- **Nature:** Cognitive biases are typically unconscious and automatic, meaning individuals may not be aware of their presence or influence on their judgments and decisions. They can manifest in various forms, such as confirmation bias, availability heuristic, anchoring bias, and more.

- **Influencing Factors:** Cognitive biases can arise from a variety of conditions or scenarios, including:

  - **Heuristics:** Mental shortcuts used for decision-making or judgments, which may simplify complex information but also lead to errors.

  - **Emotional Input:** Emotions can influence cognitive processes, leading to biased interpretations and judgments based on emotional states.

- o **Social and Peer Pressure:** The influence of social norms, expectations, and peer pressure can shape perceptions and decisions, contributing to biased thinking.

- o **Ageing:** Cognitive biases may become more pronounced with age due to changes in cognitive abilities and information processing.

- o **Flawed Memory:** Memory distortions and inaccuracies can contribute to cognitive biases, as individuals may recall information inaccurately or selectively.

- **Impact:** Cognitive biases can have both positive and negative impacts. On the positive side, they may facilitate quicker decision-making and problem-solving by providing shortcuts in processing information. However, they can also lead to poor decisions, misjudgements, and errors in reasoning, particularly when individuals are unaware of their biases or fail to account for them.

- **Awareness and Mitigation:** Recognizing and understanding cognitive biases is essential for mitigating their impact and making more informed decisions. By becoming aware of common biases and their potential effects, individuals can employ strategies to minimize bias, such as seeking diverse perspectives, challenging assumptions, and engaging in critical thinking.

In conclusion, cognitive bias represents a significant aspect of human cognition that influences decision-making processes and judgments. While cognitive biases are inherent to human thinking, awareness and mitigation strategies can help individuals navigate biases and make more rational and objective decisions in various contexts.

Understanding Implicit Prejudice Bias: Origins and Impact

Implicit prejudice bias refers to the unconscious stereotypes and attitudes that influence people's judgments and decisions based on factors such as race, religion, gender, age, disability, social class, or language. Here's an elaboration on implicit prejudice bias, including its origins and impact:

- **Definition:** Prejudice, in general, is the prejudgment or preconceived opinion that individuals may hold before receiving rational facts or information. Implicit prejudice bias specifically involves biases that operate at an unconscious level, shaping individuals' perceptions and behaviours without their conscious awareness. These biases often lead to negative or unfavourable outcomes for certain groups or individuals.

- **Factors Influencing Bias:** Implicit prejudice bias can be influenced by various factors, including societal norms, cultural influences, upbringing, personal experiences, and media portrayals. These factors contribute to the formation of unconscious stereotypes and attitudes, which then influence individuals' judgments and behaviours in subtle ways.

- **Unconscious Stereotypes and Attitudes:** Implicit prejudice bias operates at the subconscious level, meaning individuals may not be consciously aware of their biases. These biases are often ingrained in the fundamental mechanics of thought processes, making them difficult to detect or address without deliberate effort.

- **Impact:** Implicit prejudice bias can have significant negative consequences, both at the individual and societal levels. In business settings, for example, implicit biases can influence hiring decisions, promotion opportunities, customer interactions, and workplace dynamics. When decisions are made based on unconscious stereotypes rather than merit or qualifications, it can result in discrimination, inequality, and a lack of diversity and inclusion.

- **Business Costs:** Implicit prejudice bias exacts a high business cost, as it can lead to talent loss, decreased employee morale and productivity, legal risks, damage to reputation, and loss of customer trust. Organizations that fail to address implicit bias may struggle to attract and retain diverse talent, innovate effectively, and maintain a positive workplace culture.

In conclusion, implicit prejudice bias is a pervasive phenomenon that operates at the unconscious level, influencing individuals' judgments and behaviours based on unconscious stereotypes and attitudes. Recognizing and addressing implicit bias is essential for creating more inclusive and equitable environments, both within organizations and society. Efforts to raise awareness, provide training, promote diversity and inclusion, and foster empathy and understanding can help mitigate the impact of implicit bias and promote fairness and equality for all.

Understanding Contextual Bias: Impacts and Examples

Contextual bias refers to the tendency of leaders or decision-makers to make incorrect judgments or decisions based on external influences that are irrelevant or unrelated to the situation at hand. Here's an elaboration on contextual bias, including its impacts and examples:

- **Definition:** Contextual bias occurs when individuals allow external factors, such as personal beliefs, cultural influences, or situational cues, to influence their judgments or decisions in ways that may not be objectively justified. These biases can distort perceptions, leading to errors in judgment or decision-making processes.

- **Impacts:** Contextual bias can have significant impacts on various aspects of decision-making, including hiring, promotion, performance evaluation, project management, and resource allocation. When leaders are influenced by irrelevant contextual factors, it can lead to unfairness, discrimination, and inequity within organizations. Moreover, contextual bias can undermine the credibility of decision-making processes and erode trust among team members or stakeholders.

- **Examples:**

- **Educational Bias:** In educational settings, contextual bias may manifest when teachers or educators inadvertently favour certain students based on factors such as socioeconomic status, race, or gender. This bias can result in disparities in academic opportunities and outcomes for students from marginalized or underrepresented groups.

- **Research Bias:** Contextual bias can influence the design, conduct, and interpretation of research studies. For example, researchers may unintentionally introduce biases into their studies by selecting study participants from a non-representative sample or by framing research questions in a way that favours certain outcomes.

- **Forensic Bias:** In forensic analysis, contextual bias can impact the interpretation of evidence or forensic findings. For instance, forensic examiners may be influenced by contextual factors, such as preconceived beliefs or expectations, when analysing fingerprints, DNA evidence, or other forms of forensic evidence.

- **Media Bias:** Contextual bias in media and publications

can shape the narrative or portrayal of events, issues, or individuals. Media outlets may exhibit bias by selectively presenting information, framing stories in a particular way, or using language that reinforces certain stereotypes or viewpoints.

- **Judicial Bias:** In court situations, contextual bias can influence legal decisions and judgments. Judges, jurors, or legal professionals may be susceptible to bias based on factors such as personal experiences, cultural influences, or societal stereotypes, leading to unfair or discriminatory outcomes.

In conclusion, contextual bias represents a significant challenge in decision-making processes across various domains, including education, research, forensic analysis, media, and the judicial system. By raising awareness of contextual bias, implementing strategies to mitigate its effects, and promoting diversity, equity, and inclusion, organizations and institutions can strive to ensure fair and objective decision-making practices.

Understanding Conscious Bias: Characteristics and Implications

Conscious or explicit bias, often referred to as explicit bias, involves biased decisions made with full awareness and intent. Unlike unconscious biases, which operate at a subconscious level, conscious biases are deliberate and intentional actions driven by prejudiced attitudes or beliefs. Here's an elaboration on conscious bias, including its characteristics and implications. Conscious bias refers to the explicit and deliberate prejudice or discrimination against individuals or groups based on factors such as race, gender, ethnicity, religion, sexual orientation, or other personal characteristics. These biases are consciously held beliefs or attitudes that influence decision-making processes and behaviour. Lets look into the characteristics and implications in brief.

- **Characteristics:**

  - Conscious bias involves a high level of awareness or consciousness on the part of the individual exhibiting bias. The person knowingly engages in discriminatory actions or behaviours based on their prejudiced beliefs or attitudes.

  - **Intent:** Unlike unconscious biases, which may operate without the individual's awareness, conscious biases are driven by deliberate intent. The person actively chooses to discriminate against or favour certain individuals or groups based on their biased views.

  - **Malicious Intent:** Conscious biases often involve malicious or hostile intent towards the targeted individuals or groups. The person may harbour negative attitudes, stereotypes, or prejudices and intentionally act upon them to harm or disadvantage others.

- ○ **Manifestation:** Conscious biases can manifest in various forms, including verbal expressions, discriminatory behaviours, prejudiced attitudes, or biased decision-making processes. These biases may be overt or covert, depending on the individual's willingness to express their prejudiced views openly.

- **Implications:**

  - ○ **Discriminatory Practices:** Conscious biases contribute to discriminatory practices in various contexts, including employment, education, housing, healthcare, and law enforcement. Individuals or groups subjected to conscious bias may face unfair treatment, exclusion, or marginalization based on their personal characteristics.

  - ○ **Inequality and Injustice:** Conscious biases perpetuate inequality and injustice by reinforcing stereotypes, prejudices, and discriminatory attitudes. These biases undermine efforts to promote diversity, equity, and inclusion and create barriers to equal opportunities and social justice.

  - ○ **Legal and Ethical Concerns:** Conscious bias raises legal and ethical concerns regarding discrimination and human rights violations. Organizations, institutions, or individuals found guilty of engaging in conscious bias may face legal consequences, reputational damage, or public backlash.

- o **Organizational Culture:** Conscious biases can negatively impact organizational culture by fostering a hostile or discriminatory work environment. Organizations that tolerate or condone conscious bias risk damaging employee morale, productivity, and trust in leadership.

In conclusion, conscious bias represents a significant challenge to promoting diversity, equity, and inclusion in society. By raising awareness of conscious biases, implementing anti-bias training programs, and fostering a culture of respect and acceptance, individuals and organizations can work towards mitigating the harmful effects of conscious bias and promoting fairness and equality for all.

Understanding Unconscious Bias: Origins, Characteristics, and Impact

Unconscious or implicit bias refers to the automatic and unintentional biases that influence perceptions, attitudes, and behaviours towards certain social groups. Unlike conscious biases, which involve deliberate and intentional actions, unconscious biases operate outside of conscious awareness and control. Here's an elaboration on unconscious bias, including its origins, characteristics, and impact:

- **Origins:**

  - o **Implicit Stereotypes:** Unconscious bias is often rooted in implicit stereotypes, which are learned associations between qualities and social groups. These stereotypes are acquired through family, social, and educational environments, as well as cultural influences.

o **Childhood Formation:** Unconscious biases are typically formed during childhood and adolescence when individuals are exposed to various social messages, cultural norms, and societal stereotypes. These early experiences shape perceptions and attitudes towards different social groups.

o **Learned Associations:** Unconscious biases arise from learned associations between specific traits or characteristics and social categories such as race, gender, ethnicity, age, or socioeconomic status. These associations become deeply ingrained in the subconscious mind and can influence decision-making processes.

- **Characteristics:**

o **Lack of Awareness:** Unconscious biases operate outside of conscious awareness, meaning individuals may not be aware of their biases or the impact they have on their attitudes and behaviours. These biases may conflict with an individual's conscious beliefs or values.

o **Automaticity:** Unconscious biases are automatic

and reflexive, occurring rapidly and effortlessly in response to social stimuli or situational cues. Individuals may exhibit bias without deliberate thought or intention.

- o **Influence on Behaviour:** Unconscious biases can significantly influence behaviour, particularly in situations where quick decisions are required or when individuals are under stress. These biases may manifest in subtle ways, such as microaggressions, subtle forms of discrimination, or differential treatment of individuals from different social groups.

- **Impact:**

  - o **Contribution to Inequality:** Unconscious biases contribute to inequality by perpetuating stereotypes, prejudices, and discriminatory attitudes. These biases can result in unfair treatment, marginalization, or exclusion of individuals belonging to certain social groups.

  - o **Quick Decision-Making:** Unconscious biases can influence decision-making processes, leading to biased judgments or evaluations of others. In contexts such as hiring, promotions, or performance evaluations, unconscious biases may result in disparities in opportunities or outcomes.

○ **Social Dynamics:** Unconscious biases affect social interactions and dynamics by shaping interpersonal relationships, communication patterns, and group dynamics. These biases can create barriers to collaboration, diversity, and inclusion within organizations and communities.

○ **Mitigating Strategies:** Awareness and education are essential for mitigating the impact of unconscious bias. Training programs, diversity initiatives, and inclusive leadership practices can help individuals and organizations recognize and address unconscious biases to promote fairness, equity, and social justice.

In conclusion, unconscious bias represents a significant challenge to fostering diversity, equity, and inclusion in society. By raising awareness, promoting self-reflection, and implementing strategies to mitigate unconscious biases, individuals and organizations can work towards creating more inclusive and equitable environments for all.

Exploring Common Types of Unconscious Bias

Unconscious bias encompasses a wide range of biases that influence perceptions, attitudes, and behaviours towards others, often without conscious awareness. Understanding these biases is essential for fostering diversity, equity, and inclusion in various settings. Here are some of the most common types of unconscious bias:

- **Affinity Bias:**

  - **Description:** Affinity bias involves the unconscious preference for individuals who share similar qualities, interests, or backgrounds with oneself.

  - **Impact:** This bias can lead to favouritism towards those who resemble themselves, potentially excluding others who do not fit the mould.

- **Attribution Bias:**

  - **Description:** Attribution bias affects how individuals perceive their own actions versus the actions of others, often attributing success to internal factors and failure to external factors.

  - **Impact:** This bias can result in undervaluing others' accomplishments while overvaluing their mistakes, leading to unfair assessments and judgments.

- **Ageism:**

  - **Description:** Ageism involves negative attitudes or discrimination based on a person's age, particularly prevalent against older individuals in the workplace.

  - **Impact:** Ageism can lead to limited opportunities, unequal treatment, and feelings of disadvantage among older workers, particularly women.

- **Beauty Bias:**

- **Description:** Beauty bias is the tendency to perceive attractive individuals as more competent, successful, or qualified than unattractive individuals.

- **Impact:** This bias can result in unfair advantages for those perceived as physically attractive, depriving others based on superficial characteristics.

- **Confirmation Bias:**

  - **Description:** Confirmation bias involves seeking out information that confirms pre-existing beliefs or opinions while disregarding contradictory evidence.

  - **Impact:** This bias can reinforce stereotypes, limit critical thinking, and lead to narrow-minded decision-making.

- **Conformity Bias:**

  - **Description:** Conformity bias occurs when individuals adopt the views or behaviours of others to seek acceptance or approval, even if it contradicts their own beliefs.

  - **Impact:** This bias can suppress diverse perspectives, stifle innovation, and perpetuate groupthink within organizations.

- **Contrast Effect:**

  - **Description:** The contrast effect involves evaluating two or more things based on their relative differences rather than their intrinsic qualities.

- o **Impact:** This bias can distort perceptions, leading to exaggerated comparisons and inaccurate judgments.

- **Gender Bias:**

  - o **Description:** Gender bias entails favouring one gender over the other based on stereotypes or traditional gender roles.

  - o **Impact:** This bias can result in unequal treatment, limited opportunities, and barriers to gender equality in various domains.

Understanding and addressing these unconscious biases is essential for promoting fairness, inclusivity, and diversity in all aspects of society. By raising awareness, fostering empathy, and implementing strategies to mitigate bias, individuals and organizations can work towards creating more equitable and inclusive environments for everyone.

Understanding Statistical Bias in Research: Examples and Implications

Statistical bias refers to systematic errors or inaccuracies in the process of data collection, analysis, or interpretation, which can lead to misleading results or conclusions that deviate from the true representation of the population or phenomenon under study. These biases can arise at various stages of the research process and can significantly impact the validity and reliability of study findings. Here are some common examples of statistical bias:

- **Forecast Bias:**

  - **Description:** Forecast bias occurs when there is a consistent tendency for predictions or forecasts to overestimate or underestimate future outcomes.

  - **Impact:** This bias can lead to inaccurate projections and decisions, potentially resulting in financial losses or missed opportunities.

- **Observer-Expectancy Effect:**

  - **Description:** The observer-expectancy effect occurs when researchers' expectations or beliefs about the outcome of a study influence their observations or interpretations of data.

  - **Impact:** This bias can introduce unintentional bias into research findings, affecting the objectivity and reliability of the study results.

- **Selection Bias:**

  - Description: Selection bias occurs when the process of selecting participants for a study systematically excludes or includes certain individuals or groups, leading to a non-representative sample.

  - **Impact:** This bias can distort the study findings and limit the generalizability of the results to the broader population.

- **Reporting Bias:**

  - **Description:** Reporting bias occurs when there is a tendency for researchers or study participants to selectively report or publish results that are more favourable or significant, while omitting or downplaying less favorable findings.

  - **Impact:** This bias can skew the overall evidence base and lead to an overestimation of treatment effects or outcomes, potentially influencing clinical practice or policy decisions.

- **Social Desirability Bias:**

  - **Description:** Social desirability bias refers to the tendency for individuals to respond in a manner that is perceived as socially acceptable or favourable, rather than providing honest or accurate responses.

  - **Impact:** This bias can lead to inflated or distorted self-reports in surveys or questionnaires, resulting in biased estimates of attitudes, behaviours, or preferences.

Addressing statistical bias requires careful attention to research design, data collection methods, and analysis techniques to minimize or mitigate potential sources of bias. By implementing rigorous study protocols, employing randomization techniques, ensuring sample representativeness, and promoting transparency in reporting, researchers can enhance the validity and reliability of their research findings. Additionally, conducting sensitivity analyses and exploring alternative explanations can help identify and mitigate the effects of bias on study results.

Understanding Selection Bias: Observing What Stands Out

Selection bias occurs when certain individuals or elements in a population have a higher probability of being selected for a study or observation compared to others, leading to a skewed representation of the population. It can arise from various factors, such as the sampling method used, the study design, or the way data is collected.

For example, imagine a study aimed at assessing the effectiveness of a new teaching method in improving students' performance. If the selection of participants is based solely on volunteers who are already enthusiastic about the teaching method, the sample may not be representative of the entire student population. This could lead to overestimating the effectiveness of the teaching method because the sample mainly consists of students who are likely to perform well regardless of the method used.

Selection bias can also occur in observational studies, where researchers observe naturally occurring phenomena without intervening. In such cases, individuals or events that are more noticeable or memorable may receive disproportionate attention, leading to biased conclusions.

For instance, consider a study investigating the impact of social media on mental health. If researchers primarily focus on individuals who have experienced severe mental health issues because of social media use, they may overlook those who have had positive experiences or no significant effects. This could result in an exaggerated perception of social media's negative impact on mental health.

To mitigate selection bias, researchers must employ rigorous sampling methods that ensure a random and representative selection of participants from the target population. Additionally, researchers should carefully consider potential sources of bias when designing studies and interpreting results to ensure the validity and reliability of their findings.

Unveiling the Fundamental Attribution Error: Understanding Behavioural Bias

The fundamental attribution error delves into the inherent tendency of individuals to attribute the behaviour of others to internal characteristics or traits, while overlooking the influence of situational factors. This bias leads individuals to make unfair judgments about others based solely on observed behaviour, without considering the broader context.

For example, if a colleague fails to complete a task on time, one might hastily conclude that they are lazy or incompetent, failing to acknowledge potential external factors such as workload, time constraints, or personal challenges. This tendency to overlook situational factors and attribute behaviour solely to internal characteristics is the crux of the fundamental attribution error.

Conversely, when individuals find themselves in similar situations, they are quick to attribute their own behaviour to external factors rather than internal traits. For instance, if they are late to a meeting due to unforeseen circumstances like a flat tyre or traffic congestion, they readily offer these external explanations to justify their actions.

Understanding the fundamental attribution error is crucial for promoting empathy, fairness, and accurate assessments of behaviour. By recognizing this bias, individuals can strive to adopt a more nuanced perspective that considers both internal dispositions and external circumstances when evaluating the actions of others. This awareness fosters a more compassionate and inclusive approach to interpersonal interactions and decision-making processes.

Leadership and Management: Distinguishing the Key Differences

Leadership and management are often used interchangeably, but they represent distinct yet complementary aspects of organizational dynamics. Understanding the differences between the two concepts is crucial for effective organizational governance and team development.

Leadership primarily focuses on inspiring and influencing others towards a shared vision or goal. Leaders set direction, motivate team members, and foster innovation and change. They emphasize strategic thinking, vision, and long-term goals. Leadership is more about guiding and empowering individuals to reach their full potential, often by leveraging personal qualities such as charisma, emotional intelligence, and vision.

On the other hand, **management** is concerned with planning, organizing, and controlling resources to achieve specific objectives efficiently. Managers coordinate tasks, allocate resources, and ensure that operations run smoothly on a day-to-day basis. Management involves implementing strategies, establishing processes, and monitoring performance to meet short-term targets and operational needs. It emphasizes structure, stability, and consistency.

While leadership and management serve different functions, they are interdependent and complementary in achieving organizational success. Effective leadership provides direction and inspiration, while efficient management ensures that plans are executed effectively and resources are utilized optimally. In essence, leadership sets the course, while management steers the ship to reach its destination.

Leadership and management also differ in terms of their focus and scope. Leadership tends to be more visionary and people-oriented, focusing on long-term goals and inspiring individuals to excel. Management, on the other hand, is more task-oriented and process-driven, focusing on achieving short-term objectives and optimizing organizational processes.

Moreover, leadership is often associated with influence and inspiration, whereas management is associated with authority and control. Leaders influence others through their charisma, vision, and ability to inspire change, whereas managers exercise authority and control to ensure compliance with policies, procedures, and guidelines.

In summary, while leadership and management are distinct concepts, they are both essential for effective organizational functioning. Leadership provides vision, inspiration, and direction, while management ensures that plans are executed efficiently and resources are managed effectively. By recognizing and leveraging the unique strengths of both leadership and management, organizations can achieve sustainable growth, innovation, and success.

Navigating the Dynamics Between Leadership and Management

Leadership and management are often used interchangeably, but despite their overlap, significant distinctions exist between the two. While Leadership primarily focuses on inspiring the workforce and charting the company's vision and direction, Management is more concerned with executing and propelling that vision forward.

Leaders typically seek new ideas and adopt a future-oriented perspective, while Managers concentrate on implementing these ideas in the present context. Additionally, Leadership involves shaping and delineating workplace culture, whereas Management involves endorsing and fostering that culture among employees.

Despite these differences, the roles of leadership and management often intertwine. Whether one holds a formal leadership position or not, demonstrating leadership qualities is crucial for effective management. Strong communication skills, passion, problem-solving abilities, decision-making process, and crisis management skills are indispensable for both roles.

In a keynote discussion at Harvard Business School Online's annual conference, Connext, HBS Professors Nancy Koehn and Joe Fuller delved into the interplay between leadership and management. Koehn referred to the work of HBS Professor John Kotter, who aptly defined leadership as the creation of positive, non-incremental change, emphasizing the importance of vision, strategy, empowerment, and coalition-building.

Fuller, an instructor of the online course Management Essentials, contrasted management as the process of executing tasks regularly and reiterated the significance of understanding individual motivations to bring out the best in people.

While these definitions highlight parallels between leadership and management, they also underscore key differences. One such difference is the focus on Process versus Vision. Effective leadership revolves around envisioning and guiding change, whereas management revolves around achieving organizational goals through structured processes like budgeting and staffing.

HBS Dean Nitin Nohria emphasized this distinction, noting that management entails working with others to execute predefined goals, while leadership involves developing and driving the direction of those goals.

Organizing versus Aligning: In Warren Bennis's book, "On Becoming a Leader," the author delineates key disparities between managers and leaders:

- Managers administer, while leaders innovate.

- Managers maintain whereas leaders develop.

- Managers focus on systems and structure, while leaders concentrate on people.

Managers execute goals through coordinated actions and tactical processes, overseeing tasks and activities that unfold in stages to achieve specific outcomes. For instance, they may orchestrate decision-making processes during pivotal meetings or devise plans for communicating organizational changes.

In contrast, leaders prioritize aligning and influencing people rather than organizing them to complete tasks. According to HBS Professor Anthony Mayo, the central function of leadership is mobilizing others to execute individual and collective tasks. Through self-reflection and honest feedback, leaders can develop a personal leadership style that empowers employees and inspires them to believe in and pursue significant organizational initiatives.

Position versus Quality: The term "manager" typically denotes a specific role within an organization's hierarchy, whereas referring to someone as a "leader" implies a more fluid and multifaceted meaning. Leadership coach Doc Norton emphasizes that being a manager is a title and a set of responsibilities, but it does not inherently make one a leader. True leadership is demonstrated through action that inspires, encourages, or engages others, irrespective of one's title or position.

Leadership is not merely a title; it is a quality that requires cultivation. By developing emotional intelligence and mastering the art of influencing others, professionals at all levels can enhance their self-awareness and bring out the best in themselves and others.

For both seasoned and aspiring managers, possessing strong leadership skills can enhance job performance and deepen understanding of how to influence decision-making contexts and environments. Reflecting on one's management style and experiences and investing in continuous learning and skill-building are essential steps toward becoming a world-class manager.

In summary, while leadership and management share similarities, they serve distinct functions within organizations. Understanding and embodying the qualities of both roles are essential for effective organizational leadership and management.

DYNAMICS BETWEEN LEADERSHIP AND MANAGEMENT

LEADERSHIP	MANAGEMENT
• Focuses on inspiring, motivating individuals, long-term goals and organizational vison.	• Focuses on administering tasks, processes and achieving short-term objectives.
• Concerned with driving change and innvovation.	• Concerned with maintaining stability and efficiency.
• Emphasis envisioning, inspiring and empowering.	• Emphasis planning, organizing and controlling.
• Sets direction, creates a vision and guides changes	• Executes plans and ensures tasks are completed
• Prioritizes creativity and adaptability.	• Prioritizes efficiency and effectiveness.
• Develops talent, builds teams, and fosters growth.	• Manages resources and allocates them effciently
• Often associated with influence and inspiration.	• Typically associated with authroity and hierarchy.

This table provides a simplified overview of the main distinctions between management and leadership. Keep in mind that these roles often overlap, and effective organizations benefit from a balance of both managerial and leadership qualities.

03

Management

Crafting success through strategic direction and empowering leadership.

- PREEA V MANE

Management Style

Management style encompasses the way a leader interacts with and guides their team members to achieve organisational goals. It's not just a personal preference; it's a crucial aspect that can significantly impact an organisation's success. Here's why management style matters:

- **Employee Motivation and Engagement:** A management style that fosters open communication, recognition of achievements, and opportunities for growth can motivate employees to perform at their best. When employees feel valued and supported, they are more likely to be engaged and committed to their work.

- **Team Dynamics and Collaboration:** Different management styles can influence team dynamics and collaboration. For example, a democratic management style encourages participation and teamwork, while an autocratic style may stifle creativity and collaboration. Choosing the right management approach can foster a positive team environment where ideas are freely shared and collaboration flourishes.

- **Adaptability to Change:** In today's dynamic business

environment, adaptability is crucial for success. A management style that embraces change and encourages innovation can help organisations stay competitive and responsive to market shifts. Leaders who are flexible and open-minded can navigate change more effectively and lead their teams through periods of transition.

- **Conflict Resolution and Problem-Solving:** Effective management involves addressing conflicts and solving problems in a constructive manner. Different management styles may vary in their approach to conflict resolution, with some emphasising mediation and consensus-building while others prioritise decisive action. A well-balanced management style equips leaders with the skills to address conflicts promptly and find solutions that benefit the team.

- **Employee Development and Retention:** A supportive management style that invests in employee development and career growth can enhance retention rates and reduce turnover. When employees see opportunities for advancement and skill development, they are more likely to stay with the organisation and contribute to its long-term success.

Overall, management style plays a pivotal role in shaping organisational culture, driving performance, and achieving strategic objectives. By understanding the needs of their team members and adapting their management approach accordingly, leaders can create a positive work environment where employees thrive and the organisation flourishes.

The Crucial Role of Management Style in Organizational Success

Management style is paramount in shaping the success of an organisation as it profoundly impacts overall performance. A well-crafted management approach can lead to increased efficiency, heightened productivity, and superior outcomes. An ideal management style not only directs but also motivates individuals to showcase their optimal performance, thus driving the organisation towards its objectives.

Recognising the importance of management style necessitates an understanding of the diverse needs and preferences of team members. Some employees may thrive under clear direction, while others excel when given autonomy and trust. Furthermore, there are those who seek deeper meaning in their work and desire to understand how their tasks contribute to broader societal goals. By comprehending these varying needs, managers can tailor their leadership approach to suit the unique characteristics of their team members.

Flexibility is key in selecting an appropriate management style, as organisations typically encompass a mix of employee types. While some may require more hands-on guidance, others may flourish with minimal intervention. Additionally, the ability to adapt management style based on individual and situational factors ensures a balanced approach that resonates with the diverse workforce.

Management style can be elucidated through a structural framework that encompasses various dimensions such as communication, decision-making, delegation, and conflict resolution. By delineating these aspects, managers can refine their approach and effectively lead their teams towards success.

In summary, management style serves as a cornerstone of organisational effectiveness, influencing employee engagement, satisfaction, and ultimately, organisational performance. By cultivating an understanding of employee needs and leveraging a flexible leadership approach, managers can foster a culture of productivity, innovation, and growth within their organisations.

Navigating Management Styles: Flexibility, Adaptability, and Resilience in Organizational Leadership

Determining the best management style is a nuanced endeavour, as it necessitates a keen understanding of the dynamic nature of organisational needs and the diverse range of individuals within the workforce. There is no one-size-fits-all approach, as what works well in one context may prove ineffective in another. Instead, the most effective management style is one that is flexible and adaptable, capable of incorporating various approaches based on the specific requirements of different departments, hierarchies, and subject matter experts.

Rather than adhering rigidly to a single management style, leaders must possess the acumen to recognise when to apply different styles depending on the situation at hand. Factors such as organisational culture, the nature of tasks, employee skills and preferences, and overall company objectives all play crucial roles in determining the appropriate management approach.

For instance, in times of crisis, an autocratic management style may be warranted, enabling swift decision-making and immediate action to mitigate unforeseen challenges. Conversely, during periods of stability, a democratic or transformational leadership style may foster innovation, collaboration, and continuous improvement, thereby maintaining a competitive advantage in the industry.

The key takeaway is the recognition that management style should be fluid and responsive, capable of adapting to the ever-changing demands of the business landscape. By leveraging a combination of management styles tailored to the unique needs of each situation, leaders can cultivate a resilient workforce that remains agile and responsive, whether navigating through crises or pursuing ongoing growth and development initiatives.

Ultimately, the goal of an effective management style is to foster an environment of employee engagement, open communication, and alignment with organisational values and objectives. By empowering teams to leverage the strengths of various management approaches, leaders can unlock their full potential and drive sustained success for the organisation.

The Impact of Visionary Leadership in Luxury Brand Management

Visionary leadership is a transformative force within luxury brand management, inspiring teams to exceed expectations and embody the company's overarching vision. A visionary leader possesses the ability to articulate a compelling common purpose, fostering a sense of unity and direction among team members. Through effective communication, they paint a vivid picture of the organisation's future, igniting passion and commitment among their followers.

In the realm of luxury brand management, visionary leadership serves as a catalyst for innovation and excellence. By instilling a shared sense of purpose, visionary managers empower their teams to embrace challenges and strive for excellence. Rather than resorting to micromanagement, they entrust their staff with autonomy, allowing them to leverage their unique strengths and creativity to achieve collective goals.

Central to the visionary management approach is the cultivation of trust and support within the team. Visionary leaders demonstrate unwavering trust in their team members' abilities, providing them with the freedom to explore new ideas and approaches. They offer constructive feedback and abundant praise, nurturing a culture of growth and recognition.

By embracing visionary management principles, luxury brand management teams feel valued, trusted, and motivated to excel. Autonomy, encouragement, and acknowledgement of achievements foster a sense of ownership and pride among employees, driving them to go the extra mile in pursuit of the company's vision. Ultimately, visionary leadership plays a pivotal role in shaping a positive and high-performing work environment within the luxury brand management industry.

The Impact of Coaching Management Style on Employee Growth and Performance

Coaching management style is rooted in the desire to help individuals reach their full potential and perform at their best. This approach focuses on fostering growth and development among employees, prioritising long-term learning and improvement over short-term outcomes. By providing guidance, support, and opportunities for skill enhancement, coaching managers empower their teams to constantly evolve, deliver high-quality service, and take on additional responsibilities.

One of the key aspects of coaching management is the emphasis on individual growth and development. Managers in this role actively identify the strengths, areas for improvement, and specific development goals of each employee. Through open communication, active listening, and constructive feedback, they create a supportive environment where employees feel encouraged to explore their potential and pursue personal and professional growth opportunities.

Central to the coaching approach is the concept of empowerment. Managers act as facilitators, guiding employees to identify and solve problems on their own while aiding and support as needed. This approach instils a sense of ownership and accountability among employees, fostering a culture of self-reliance and continuous learning.

Moreover, the coaching management style cultivates strong relationships between managers and their teams. By demonstrating genuine care and interest in their employees' development, managers build trust and rapport, leading to higher levels of engagement and motivation. This supportive environment not only drives individual success but also contributes to overall organisational performance.

By investing in the growth and development of their team members, coaching managers create a pipeline of future leaders and ensure the long-term success of the organisation. Through continuous learning, skill-building, and opportunities for advancement, employees are empowered to excel in their roles and contribute to the company's growth trajectory.

In conclusion, coaching management style fosters a culture of continuous improvement, collaboration, and long-term performance excellence. By prioritising employee growth and development, coaching managers unlock the full potential of their teams, driving success at both individual and organisational levels.

The Impact of Autocratic Management Style on Employee Engagement and Performance

Autocratic management style operates on a hierarchical, top-down approach where decision-making is centralised at the top levels of the organisation, with little to no input from team members. Managers in this style delegate tasks downward and expect strict obedience from employees without room for collaboration or feedback.

In an autocratic management setting, employees are expected to follow directives without question, with little opportunity for creativity or open dialogue. Managers wield significant power and make decisions independently, often relying on fear, guilt, or shame as motivators rather than positive reinforcement. This approach tends to result in low morale, diminished innovation, and high staff turnover, as employees feel disempowered and undervalued.

While autocratic management can lead to quick decision-making and streamlined processes, it often comes at the expense of employee engagement and creativity. Employees may feel stifled and demotivated, leading to reduced productivity and loyalty. While some individuals may prefer clear instructions and directives, high-performing and creative employees may struggle to thrive in an environment where their input is disregarded.

It's essential for organisations to recognise the limitations of autocratic management and adopt a more balanced approach that considers employee engagement and involvement. While certain situations may warrant a more directive style, it's crucial to strike a balance between authority and collaboration to foster a positive work environment and encourage employee growth and development.

Ultimately, autocratic management should be used sparingly and with caution, as its long-term impact on employee morale and performance can be detrimental to organisational success. By prioritising open communication, employee empowerment, and a supportive leadership approach, organisations can create a culture that values and respects the contributions of all team members.

Empowering Change: The Impact of Transformational Management Style

Transformational management style is characterised by a forward-thinking approach that prioritises innovation and growth to keep pace with evolving customer demands. Managers employing this style are catalysts for change, constantly challenging their teams to adapt and improve, pushing them beyond perceived limitations.

At its core, transformational management is about empowering individuals to achieve extraordinary results. Managers in this role recognise and leverage the skills and talents of their team members, encouraging them to think creatively and explore new possibilities. By instilling a sense of belief and confidence, transformational leaders inspire their teams to strive for excellence and consistently raise the bar for performance.

One of the key aspects of transformational management is its focus on fostering a culture of innovation and continuous learning. Leaders in this style promote an environment where employees feel encouraged to challenge themselves and pursue personal growth. By nurturing a spirit of creativity and curiosity, managers cultivate a workforce that is not only adaptable but also resilient in the face of change.

Transformational leaders lead by example, displaying charisma, enthusiasm, and a genuine passion for the organisation's mission. Through open communication and mutual respect, they build strong relationships with their team members, acting as mentors who recognise and nurture individual strengths and potential.

While transformational management can yield significant benefits, such as increased employee engagement and sustainable long-term success, it also comes with its challenges. Managers must strike a balance, avoiding pushing their teams too hard or spreading them too thinly. When executed effectively, however, transformational management can drive positive change, inspire personal growth, and foster a sense of purpose and fulfillment among employees.

In essence, the transformational management style is not just about achieving short-term goals; it's about inspiring and empowering individuals to reach their full potential, driving organisational success, and shaping a brighter future for all stakeholders involved.

The Transactional Approach: Balancing Rewards and Consequences

In a transactional management style, interactions between managers and employees are viewed as transactions akin to a quid pro quo arrangement—where one party provides something in exchange for another's cooperation or performance. While this approach may initially motivate through incentives and rewards, such as financial bonuses, its effectiveness tends to diminish over time, leading to decreased employee engagement.

Transactional managers operate within a structured framework, focusing on implementing processes with clear goals and performance metrics. Tasks are treated as transactions that necessitate completion for predetermined rewards or consequences. This style emphasises the establishment of well-defined expectations and provides tangible incentives, such as bonuses, commissions, or promotions, for meeting or exceeding targets. Conversely, disciplinary measures may be applied for failing to meet expectations.

While transactional management can be effective in organisations with routine tasks or when immediate performance improvement is needed, it may not foster long-term employee engagement or creativity. This is because motivation is primarily linked to extrinsic rewards and consequences rather than intrinsic factors like personal growth or a sense of purpose. Furthermore, in dynamic and rapidly changing environments, this approach may prove ineffective, as it prioritises maintaining order over adaptation and innovation.

Transactional leadership, characterised by contingent rewards and punishments, focuses on achieving short-term objectives through management by exception—intervening only when standards are not met. While this approach may offer short-term gains in performance, its reliance on transactional exchanges may undermine employee morale and hinder long-term organisational success.

Therefore, while transactional management can provide structure and clarity in certain contexts, it must be adopted carefully, and its limitations must be acknowledged. To cultivate sustained employee engagement and drive innovation, organisations are encouraged to complement transactional approaches with strategies that emphasise intrinsic motivation, employee involvement in decision-making, and a shared sense of purpose. Ultimately, a balanced approach that combines transactional elements with a focus on empowerment and inspiration is essential for fostering a thriving organisational culture.

The Power of Collaboration: Embracing Democratic Management

In democratic or participative management, the principles of democracy are applied to the workplace, emphasising the inclusion of employees in decision-making processes. Unlike autocratic styles, where decisions are made unilaterally by management, democratic managers recognise the value of their team's diverse perspectives and experiences, actively involving them in shaping the direction of the organisation.

This management style promotes a collaborative work environment characterised by open communication channels and a culture of shared decision-making. Employees are encouraged to contribute their ideas, opinions, expertise, and knowledge, which are then considered in the decision-making process. While the final decision rests with the manager, involving staff in the process fosters a sense of ownership and commitment to the outcomes.

The democratic approach not only boosts morale but also strengthens trust and relationships within the team. By making employees feel valued and respected, democratic managers create an environment where individuals are motivated to work hard towards common goals. This style of management cultivates a sense of belonging, shared responsibility, empowerment, and accountability among team members, leading to increased engagement and job satisfaction.

Moreover, a democratic work environment nurtures creativity and innovation. By providing opportunities for employees to contribute their ideas and participate in decision-making, organisations tap into the collective intelligence of their workforce. This fosters a culture of innovation, where employees feel encouraged to experiment, take risks, and explore new ways of doing things. As a result, organisations that embrace democratic management benefit from enhanced adaptability, resilience, and efficiency.

While democratic decision-making may be slower compared to autocratic styles, its impact is significant in environments that require flexibility, creativity, and continuous improvement. By promoting collaboration and teamwork, democratic management enables organisations to harness the full potential of their employees and achieve shared objectives.

In conclusion, the democratic management style serves as a powerful tool for bringing colleagues together, fostering collaboration, and aligning efforts towards the goals of the business. By embracing inclusivity and valuing employee input, organisations can create a supportive and dynamic work environment that drives innovation, productivity, and success.

Navigating Conflict: The Collaborative Approach to Conflict Management

Conflict management styles play a crucial role in handling disagreements and disputes within organisations, requiring effective communication and leadership skills to navigate tense situations. Among these styles, the collaborative approach stands out as a method for fostering open dialogue, mutual understanding, and long-term solutions.

At its core, the collaborative style emphasises active listening, empathy, and the identification of underlying issues to facilitate respectful communication among team members. Managers employing this approach prioritise maintaining harmony and relationships, recognising the importance of addressing conflicts promptly to prevent escalation and maintain productivity.

Accommodative in nature, managers utilising the collaborative style seek to find a middle ground and encourage compromise among conflicting parties. They understand that resolving conflicts requires a willingness to accommodate the needs and perspectives of all involved, even if it means making concessions or sacrificing personal interests.

Central to the collaborative approach is the promotion of open communication and problem-solving. Managers encourage team members to engage in constructive dialogue, fostering an environment where concerns can be addressed and solutions explored collaboratively. By emphasising a win-win mindset, managers aim to reach mutually acceptable resolutions that promote teamwork, trust, and long-term success.

While the collaborative style is effective in situations where immediate resolution is necessary, it also fosters a culture of transparency, accountability, and empowerment. By involving stakeholders in the decision-making process and valuing their input, managers build trust and cohesion within the team, ultimately driving organisational success.

In summary, the collaborative approach to conflict management offers a framework for resolving disputes through open dialogue, compromise, and mutual understanding. By prioritising effective communication and problem-solving, managers can foster a culture of collaboration and teamwork that leads to sustainable solutions and positive outcomes.

Embracing Autonomy: The Laissez-faire Management Style

Laissez-faire management, derived from the French term meaning "let it be," embodies a hands-off approach where managers provide minimal direction and interference, entrusting significant autonomy to their teams. While this style can empower highly skilled and motivated individuals, it also presents challenges if not implemented effectively.

In the laissez-faire approach, managers refrain from micromanagement and instead delegate decision-making authority and responsibilities to employees, allowing them the freedom to operate independently. This autonomy is particularly beneficial for self-motivated individuals and subject matter experts who excel when given the opportunity to apply their knowledge and skills creatively.

However, the laissez-faire style can lead to challenges such as a lack of guidance, shared vision, and supervision. Without adequate support and direction, employees may feel neglected, unsure of expectations, and ineffective in achieving goals. Additionally, the risk of last-minute non-delivery due to dependency on individual expertise exists, posing potential setbacks for timely completion.

Despite these challenges, when implemented carefully with clear communication and well-defined goals, the laissez-faire style fosters creativity, accountability, confidence, and trust among team members. It promotes collaboration, autonomy, and self-motivation, ultimately contributing to a resilient and high-performing workforce.

However, it's crucial for managers to strike a balance and avoid complete disengagement, as unchecked autonomy can lead to disorganisation, missed deadlines, and reduced productivity. Therefore, while embracing autonomy is essential, it's equally important for managers to provide necessary support, resources, and guidance to ensure success within a laissez-faire management framework.

Key Strengths and Challenges

Strengths and challenges in management encompass a broad spectrum of factors that influence organisational effectiveness and leadership efficacy. Recognising and leveraging strengths while addressing challenges is essential for achieving optimal performance and fostering growth within teams and organisations.

Strengths in management often include effective communication skills, strategic thinking, decision-making process, and the ability to inspire and motivate teams towards shared goals. These strengths enable managers to articulate visions, allocate resources efficiently, and navigate complex challenges with resilience and agility. Moreover, adept managers excel in fostering collaboration, building cohesive teams, and cultivating a positive work culture that fosters innovation and productivity.

However, alongside these strengths, managers also face a myriad of challenges that can impede their effectiveness and hinder organisational progress. Common challenges in management may include:

- **Resistance to Change:** Implementing organisational change initiatives can be met with resistance from employees who are reluctant to embrace new processes or ways of working. Managing this resistance while driving change is a delicate balancing act for managers.

- **Conflict Resolution:** Managing conflicts and interpersonal disputes within teams requires strong mediation skills and emotional intelligence. Failure to address conflicts effectively can lead to decreased morale, productivity, and team cohesion.

- **Time Management:** Managers often juggle multiple responsibilities and priorities, making effective time management essential for maximising productivity and achieving strategic objectives. Balancing competing demands while maintaining focus on key priorities can be challenging.

- **Employee Engagement:** Sustaining high levels of employee engagement and motivation requires continuous effort from managers. Building trust, providing meaningful feedback, and recognising employee contributions are vital for fostering a positive work environment.

- **Performance Management:** Effectively evaluating and managing employee performance is critical for driving individual and organisational success. Setting clear expectations, providing regular feedback, and offering opportunities for growth and development are key components of effective performance management.

- **Adapting to Change:** In today's dynamic business environment, managers must be adaptable and responsive to evolving market trends, technological advancements, and industry disruptions. Flexibility and agility are essential for navigating uncertainty and driving organisational resilience.

- **Work-Life Balance:** Achieving a healthy work-life balance is a perennial challenge for many managers. Balancing professional responsibilities with personal well-being is essential for preventing burnout and maintaining long-term job satisfaction and performance.

Overall, while management strengths empower leaders to drive organisational success, addressing challenges effectively is crucial for overcoming obstacles and fostering continuous improvement and growth. By leveraging strengths, proactively addressing challenges, and cultivating a culture of learning and innovation, managers can enhance their effectiveness and contribute to sustainable organisational success.

Mastering Reliability: The Key Strengths of Effective Management

Reliability in management encapsulates the ability of managers to consistently deliver results by ensuring that their teams fulfil tasks and meet deadlines effectively. It reflects their capacity to maintain a strong work ethic and dependability, which in turn earns trust from senior leadership. When a manager is reliable, they demonstrate a commitment to excellence and accountability, instilling confidence that they can successfully execute projects with minimal instruction or oversight. This strength not only fosters a sense of reliability within the team but also showcases the manager's capability to handle responsibilities efficiently, thereby enhancing their reputation as a dependable leader.

Organisational Mastery: The Backbone of Effective Management

Effective managers possess the strength of organisation, a skill that enables them to maintain control and clarity amidst the complexities of projects or processes. By being keenly aware of every detail, they ensure that teams stay on track to meet deadlines and fulfil expectations. This strength is pivotal in preventing crucial information or elements from slipping through the cracks, thereby averting potential gaps or oversights that could impede progress. In essence, organisational prowess serves as the backbone of effective management, facilitating smooth operations and successful outcomes.

Motivational Mastery: Igniting Team Passion and Performance

A cornerstone of effective management lies in its ability to inspire and motivate teams to perform at their peak. Motivational managers exude enthusiasm and passion for their work and values, serving as catalysts for their team's energy and drive. They go beyond conventional thinking, consistently generating innovative ideas that inject excitement and vitality into the workplace. Moreover, these managers extend unwavering support and encouragement to their teams, fostering an environment where every individual feels empowered to excel. By mastering the art of motivation, managers not only ignite the passion within their teams but also unlock their full potential, driving performance and achieving outstanding results.

Mastering Problem-Solving: Unleashing Innovative Solutions and Cohesive Teams

Problem-solving prowess is a hallmark of effective management, characterised by a solution-oriented mindset that navigates through ongoing challenges and anticipated hurdles with finesse. Managers adept in problem-solving possess the remarkable ability to dissect complex situations, meticulously analyse them, and pinpoint the most effective strategies for resolution. Their strength lies in their capacity to conceive creative and practical solutions, breathing new life into age-old problems with fresh perspectives and innovative approaches.

Moreover, this skill transcends mere troubleshooting, playing a pivotal role in fostering team cohesion and synergy. By actively engaging team members in the problem-solving process, managers not only harness diverse perspectives but also cultivate a collaborative environment where each individual feels valued and empowered. Through their mastery of problem-solving, managers not only overcome obstacles but also cultivate a culture of innovation and unity, propelling their teams towards unprecedented success.

Embracing Flexibility: Navigating Change with Agile Leadership

Flexibility stands as a cornerstone of effective leadership, enabling managers to adeptly navigate the ever-shifting landscapes of modern work environments. Managers endowed with this strength demonstrate a remarkable capacity to adapt swiftly to changing regulations, unforeseen circumstances, and dynamic work environments. Rather than being derailed by unexpected challenges, they embrace change as an opportunity for growth and innovation, leveraging their ability to swiftly learn and evolve to maintain productivity and efficiency.

One of the hallmarks of flexible leadership lies in the manager's aptitude for quick learning and adaptation. Whether it's mastering new technologies, embracing novel methodologies, or staying abreast of industry developments, these leaders display a comfort and eagerness in embracing change. Their openness to innovation and willingness to explore new avenues empower them to lead their teams towards greater success in an ever-evolving landscape.

Moreover, flexible managers serve as beacons of resilience and agility within their organisations. By embodying adaptability and embracing change with grace, they inspire confidence among their teams and foster a culture of innovation and continuous improvement. In essence, flexibility emerges as a potent asset in the arsenal of effective leaders, enabling them to navigate uncertainty with confidence and steer their teams towards enduring success.

Dedication to Excellence: Elevating Performance and Fostering Growth

Managers who exemplify a commitment to excellence epitomise the essence of effective leadership, driven by unwavering standards of quality and a relentless pursuit of superior outcomes. Their ascent to leadership positions often stems from a foundation of exacting standards and a steadfast dedication to producing work of the highest calibre. With a keen eye for detail and an innate drive for excellence, these managers consistently achieve and surpass established goals and benchmarks, setting a precedent for exceptional performance within their teams and organisations.

Central to their leadership approach is a profound understanding of how to cultivate a culture of excellence and inspire peak performance among team members. By leveraging their own strengths and abilities, these managers adeptly elevate the performance of their teams, harnessing individual talents and fostering collaborative synergy to achieve collective success. Through mentorship, guidance, and strategic direction, they empower team members to unlock their full potential and strive for excellence in every endeavour.

Furthermore, managers committed to excellence possess a relentless commitment to continuous improvement and growth. They embrace challenges as opportunities for learning and refinement, constantly seeking innovative solutions and pushing the boundaries of possibility. Their unwavering dedication to excellence serves as a catalyst for organisational advancement, driving sustained progress and propelling their teams towards unparalleled success.

In essence, a commitment to excellence lies at the heart of effective leadership, guiding managers to uphold the highest standards of performance, inspire greatness in others, and chart a course towards enduring success and distinction.

Collaborative Leadership: Fostering Teamwork for Collective Success

In the realm of management, teamwork emerges as a cornerstone principle that underpins effective leadership and organisational success. At its essence, teamwork encapsulates the collaborative synergy between managers, employees, and fellow leaders, where collective efforts converge to drive innovation, solve complex problems, and cultivate a culture of shared success.

Managers who champion teamwork recognise the inherent value of collaboration and actively engage with their teams to harness the collective intelligence and diverse perspectives within their midst. By fostering an inclusive environment where every voice is heard and valued, these leaders empower individuals to contribute their unique insights and expertise, thereby enriching the decision-making process and enhancing problem-solving capabilities.

Moreover, teamwork engenders a spirit of camaraderie and mutual support within the organisational ecosystem, fostering stronger interpersonal bonds and cultivating a sense of unity and cohesion among team members. Through collaborative endeavours and shared victories, managers cultivate a positive and nurturing work environment that fuels motivation, boosts morale, and fosters a sense of belonging among employees.

In addition, the collaborative nature of teamwork fosters a culture of continuous learning and innovation, where ideas are freely exchanged and creativity flourishes. By encouraging open dialogue and the exploration of new ideas, managers unleash the full potential of their teams, driving breakthrough innovation and propelling the organisation towards new heights of success.

Ultimately, teamwork stands as a testament to the power of collective effort and collaboration in driving organisational excellence. As managers embrace the principles of collaborative leadership, they pave the way for more positive and productive teams, forging a pathway towards shared success and enduring prosperity.

Leading with Optimism: Cultivating Positivity in Management

Optimism emerges as a foundational strength in effective management, serving as a guiding beacon that illuminates the path towards success and fosters a culture of positivity within the organisational framework. Managers who embody optimism radiate a contagious sense of hope and enthusiasm, instilling confidence in their teams and inspiring them to strive for greatness.

At its core, optimism fuels motivation and elevates performance by nurturing a belief in the inherent potential for success, both individually and collectively. By maintaining a positive outlook on the capabilities and achievements of their team members, managers cultivate a supportive environment where employees feel empowered to unleash their full potential and achieve extraordinary results.

Moreover, optimism fosters a shared vision of success among managers and their teams, aligning everyone towards common goals and objectives. By painting a compelling picture of the future and articulating a clear pathway to achievement, optimistic leaders galvanise their teams to work collaboratively towards a brighter tomorrow, united by a sense of purpose and collective ambition.

In times of change and uncertainty, the value of optimism becomes even more pronounced, serving as a beacon of hope amidst turbulence. By remaining steadfast in their belief that challenges are opportunities in disguise, optimistic managers inspire resilience and fortitude in their teams, guiding them through adversity with unwavering confidence and resolve.

Furthermore, optimism fosters a culture of innovation and creativity, encouraging individuals to embrace new ideas and approaches with a sense of curiosity and possibility. By reframing setbacks as learning experiences and celebrating progress along the journey, optimistic managers create an environment where experimentation and growth flourish, driving continuous improvement and innovation.

In essence, optimism stands as a powerful force for driving positive change and transformation within organisations. As managers cultivate a mindset of optimism and resilience, they pave the way for enhanced motivation, collaboration, and performance, propelling their teams towards greater success and fulfilment.

Overcoming Resistance to Change: Embracing Adaptability in Management

The inability to change represents a significant weakness in management, characterised by a reluctance to embrace new ideas, strategies, or approaches due to a sense of complacency and resistance to stepping outside the comfort zone. Managers afflicted by this weakness may be anchored in familiar routines and methodologies, hesitant to explore uncharted territories or disrupt established norms. However, to truly excel as an effective manager, it is imperative to cultivate adaptability and openness to change, recognising that innovation and evolution are essential for organisational growth and success.

At its core, the reluctance to change often stems from a fear of the unknown and a desire to maintain the status quo. Managers may feel comfortable operating within familiar frameworks that have served them well in the past but fail to recognise the dynamic nature of today's business landscape, where agility and flexibility are paramount. By clinging to outdated practices and resisting change, managers risk stagnation and irrelevance in an increasingly competitive environment.

To overcome this weakness, managers must cultivate a mindset of openness and receptivity to new ideas and perspectives. Instead of viewing change as a threat, they should embrace it as an opportunity for growth and innovation. This requires a willingness to challenge existing assumptions, experiment with novel approaches, and adapt to evolving circumstances. By fostering a culture of continuous learning and improvement, managers can inspire their teams to embrace change as a catalyst for progress and development.

Moreover, effective managers actively seek out opportunities for professional development and self-improvement, recognising that personal growth is essential for professional success. They engage in ongoing training, networking, and skill-building activities to expand their knowledge base and enhance their capabilities. By remaining curious, adaptable, and open-minded, managers can position themselves as dynamic leaders capable of navigating change with confidence and resilience.

Ultimately, the ability to change represents a critical competency for effective management in today's fast-paced and ever-evolving business landscape. By embracing adaptability and flexibility, managers can unlock new opportunities, drive innovation, and lead their teams to greater heights of success and achievement.

Mitigating Micromanagement: Cultivating Trust and Empowerment in Leadership

Micromanagement, a common pitfall in managerial leadership, entails excessive control and close oversight of employees' tasks and activities. While this management style may stem from a desire for perfection or a lack of trust, its detrimental effects on workplace dynamics cannot be understated. Micromanaging stifles autonomy, creativity, and growth among team members, undermining morale and productivity. To combat this tendency, it is essential for managers to foster an environment of trust, empowerment, and collaboration.

At its core, micromanagement reflects a lack of confidence in employees' abilities to perform their duties effectively without constant supervision. This approach not only erodes trust between managers and their teams but also hampers employees' sense of ownership and accountability for their work. Instead of micromanaging, managers should demonstrate confidence in their team members' capabilities and provide them with the autonomy and flexibility to execute tasks in their own way.

Effective leadership involves striking a balance between providing guidance and allowing room for individual initiative and creativity. Rather than dictating every step of the process, managers should focus on setting clear expectations, outlining goals and objectives, and then empowering employees to take ownership of their work. By fostering a culture of autonomy and empowerment, managers can inspire creativity, innovation, and initiative among team members.

Furthermore, micromanagement often leads to employee disengagement and frustration, as individuals feel undervalued and constrained in their roles. To counteract this, managers should prioritise open communication, actively listen to employee feedback, and involve team members in decision-making processes. By soliciting input and ideas from employees, managers not only demonstrate respect for their expertise but also foster a sense of ownership and investment in the team's goals and objectives.

Ultimately, mitigating micromanagement requires a shift in mindset from control to trust and empowerment. Managers must relinquish the need for constant oversight and instead focus on building strong relationships, fostering collaboration, and empowering employees to achieve their full potential. By embracing a leadership approach rooted in trust, autonomy, and empowerment, managers can create a more positive and productive work environment where team members feel valued, motivated, and empowered to succeed.

Inclusive Management

Inclusive Management: Fostering Diversity, Equity, and Collaboration

In today's interconnected world, inclusive management has emerged as a critical imperative for organisations seeking to leverage the diverse talents and perspectives of their workforce. At its essence, inclusive management entails creating a workplace environment where all individuals, regardless of race, religion, gender, or other differences, feel valued, respected, and empowered to contribute their unique insights and abilities.

Inclusive management goes beyond mere tolerance or acceptance of diversity; it actively promotes equity, access, and opportunity for all employees. By breaking down barriers and challenging stereotypes, inclusive management fosters a culture of fairness and inclusion where every individual has an equal chance to succeed and thrive.

A key principle of inclusive management is the elimination of discrimination and bias in all its forms. This involves creating policies and practices that promote equal treatment and opportunity for all employees, regardless of their background or identity. By actively addressing unconscious biases and promoting diversity awareness, inclusive management helps to create a more equitable and inclusive workplace for everyone.

Inclusive management also cultivates empathy and understanding among colleagues, fostering a sense of belonging and community within the organisation. When employees feel valued and respected for who they are, they are more likely to collaborate effectively, share ideas, and innovate together to achieve common goals.

Effective inclusive leaders lead by example, demonstrating a commitment to diversity, equity, and inclusion in their words and actions. They recognise and challenge their own biases, listen actively to diverse perspectives, and create opportunities for all employees to contribute and grow. By fostering a culture of openness, trust, and respect, inclusive leaders inspire their teams to perform at their best and achieve greater levels of success.

Organisations can implement a range of initiatives to promote inclusive management, including training programs, mentorship opportunities, and open channels of communication. By investing in diversity and inclusion initiatives, organisations can create a more positive and supportive work environment, leading to higher levels of employee engagement, satisfaction, and retention.

In summary, inclusive management is about more than just compliance or lip service to diversity; it is about creating a culture of belonging, respect, and collaboration where every individual can thrive and contribute to the organisation's success. By embracing inclusive management practices, organisations can unlock the full potential of their diverse workforce and drive sustainable growth and innovation.

Eliminating Bias: Building a Culture of Diversity and Inclusion

In today's diverse workplaces, leaders play a critical role in fostering an environment free from discrimination and bias. It is imperative for leaders to actively rule out any form of discrimination based on factors such as race, age, gender, disability, or ethnicity. Even unintentional comments or actions can have a detrimental impact on organisational culture, leading to decreased morale, productivity, and employee satisfaction.

Creating equality in diversity requires leaders to increase their awareness of their own personal biases and implement behaviour changes that promote fairness and inclusivity. This begins with self-reflection and introspection to identify and acknowledge any implicit biases that may influence decision-making or interactions with others. By recognising these biases, leaders can take proactive steps to mitigate their impact and ensure fair treatment for all individuals.

Open communication channels and safe spaces for dialogue are essential for creating an environment where employees feel comfortable expressing their thoughts and concerns without fear of judgment or reprisal. Leaders should encourage honest conversations about diversity and inclusion, actively listen to the perspectives of others, and address any instances of bias or discrimination promptly and effectively.

Additionally, leaders can challenge stereotypes and promote inclusivity by spending time with individuals from diverse backgrounds and actively seeking out diverse perspectives and experiences. By broadening their own understanding of different cultures, identities, and perspectives, leaders can cultivate a more inclusive mindset and create a workplace where everyone feels valued and respected.

Inclusive leaders understand that confronting unconscious biases is an ongoing process that requires continuous learning and self-reflection. By committing to ongoing education and training on diversity and inclusion topics, leaders can develop the skills and awareness needed to create a more equitable and inclusive workplace for all employees.

In summary, eliminating bias and building a culture of diversity and inclusion requires proactive leadership and a commitment to promoting fairness, respect, and equality for all individuals. By fostering open dialogue, challenging stereotypes, and confronting unconscious biases, leaders can create a workplace where everyone can thrive and succeed, regardless of their background or identity.

Fostering Belonging: Cultivating an Inclusive Workplace Culture

Creating a sense of belonging in the workplace is essential for fostering a culture of inclusivity and respect. Leaders play a pivotal role in inspiring individuals to transcend societal stereotypes and biases, allowing them to feel valued, respected, and empowered to contribute their unique perspectives and talents.

To cultivate a sense of belonging, leaders must create an environment where people feel comfortable being their authentic selves and expressing their thoughts and opinions without fear of judgment or prejudice. This requires promoting open communication, active listening, and mutual respect among team members, fostering a culture of acceptance and appreciation for diversity.

Training programs and awareness workshops can help raise awareness of unconscious biases and promote empathy and understanding among team members. Leading by example, demonstrating humility, and modelling inclusive behaviour are crucial for setting the tone for an inclusive workplace culture.

In addition, leaders can create opportunities for employees to connect with one another, such as through buddy programs, team-building activities, and cross-functional projects. By fostering collaboration and teamwork, leaders can break down barriers and promote a sense of camaraderie and mutual support.

It's important to recognise that creating a sense of belonging is not just about making people feel comfortable—it's also about promoting mental well-being and fostering a positive work environment. Employees who feel a sense of belonging are more likely to be engaged, motivated, and productive, leading to better overall organisational performance and customer satisfaction.

While building a culture of belonging may take time and effort, the long-term benefits are well worth it. By prioritising inclusivity and creating a workplace where every individual feels valued and respected, leaders can create a positive and supportive environment where employees can thrive and succeed.

Nurturing Empathetic Leadership Across Organisational Levels

Empathetic leadership is a vital aspect of organisational culture that extends beyond just the highest echelons of leadership. Leaders at various levels and in different roles within the organisation hold the responsibility of fostering a positive and nurturing environment where empathy thrives.

Leaders across hierarchies play a pivotal role in cultivating empathy within their teams and departments. By demonstrating empathy in their interactions and decision-making processes, leaders can strengthen relationships, facilitate conflict resolution, boost team morale, and enhance overall productivity.

It's important for leaders to recognise that empathy is not merely a leadership style but a dynamic force that drives positive change within teams and organisations. When leaders prioritise empathy, they create an environment where team members feel valued, understood, and supported, leading to increased engagement and collaboration.

Embracing empathy not only benefits individual leaders in their personal and professional growth but also contributes to the collective success of the team and organisation. By fostering a culture of empathy, leaders can inspire their teams to achieve greater heights of success and create a workplace where everyone feels empowered to thrive.

Essential Characteristics of Inclusive Leaders

- **Self-awareness:** Inclusive leaders possess a keen sense of self-awareness, allowing them to recognise and acknowledge their unconscious biases. By understanding their own perspectives and predispositions, they can approach decision-making with objectivity and fairness. Leaders must establish procedures and structures within the organisation to mitigate bias and promote impartiality, fostering a culture where employees can approach situations without subjective bias.

- **Cultural awareness and intelligence:** In a diverse workforce, cultural understanding is crucial for inclusive leaders. They demonstrate openness and a willingness to learn about different cultures, adapting their communication style and behaviour accordingly. By being mindful of cultural norms and sensitivities, leaders ensure that their messages resonate neutrally and inspire all team members, regardless of their cultural background.

- **Trust builders:** Trust is the foundation of any successful relationship, and inclusive leaders prioritise building trust within their teams. By fostering an environment of trust, leaders empower their team members to work with honesty, loyalty, and confidence. This trust enables employees to share their thoughts, opinions, and suggestions openly, leading to greater innovation, problem-solving, and risk-taking. In a transparent and trusting work environment, employees feel supported to go above and beyond to achieve their goals, contributing to the organisation's success.

- **Offering new opportunities:** Inclusive leaders understand the importance of offering new opportunities and responsibilities to different individuals within the organisation. By distributing important tasks and assignments fairly, leaders demonstrate their trust in their team members' abilities and commitment. This practice not only enhances trust but also fosters a culture of growth, development, and inclusivity, ultimately leading to a more productive and dynamic workforce.

Promoting Authenticity in Organisational Culture

Encouraging authenticity within the organisational culture is vital for fostering a work environment where individuals feel liberated from the pressure to conform to certain norms or expectations. Authenticity enables employees to express themselves genuinely while upholding professionalism and cultivating a friendly atmosphere.

By promoting authenticity, leaders set a precedent for their teams to embrace their true selves, allowing them to bring their unique perspectives, skills, and personalities to problem-solving and daily tasks. This genuine expression of self encourages creativity and innovation, as team members feel empowered to approach challenges with authenticity and originality.

Furthermore, promoting authenticity builds trust within relationships, both between leaders and team members and among colleagues. When individuals feel comfortable being themselves and expressing their thoughts and ideas authentically, trust flourishes, leading to stronger connections and collaborations.

Empowering team members to be authentic also contributes to their sense of ownership and engagement. When individuals are encouraged to be themselves, they feel valued and respected, which enhances their motivation and commitment to their work and the organisation.

In essence, promoting authenticity in the workplace creates a culture that values individuality, fosters innovation, builds trust, and empowers employees to bring their best selves to their professional endeavours.

Fostering a Collaborative Work Environment

Creating a collaborative environment within the workplace is essential for promoting innovation, providing learning opportunities, nurturing healthy relationships, and fostering a team spirit. Here's how leaders can cultivate such an environment:

- **Active Listening:** Encourage managers to practice active listening by attentively listening to team members and seeking to understand their emotions, concerns, and perspectives. This demonstrates respect and validates the importance of each team member's input.

- **Open Communication:** Encourage team members to share their thoughts and feelings openly by asking open-ended questions that invite them to elaborate. This promotes transparency, trust, and a sense of inclusion within the team.

- **Perspective-Taking:** Encourage teams to practice perspective-taking by empathising with their colleagues and trying to see situations from their viewpoint. This helps foster understanding, empathy, and collaboration among team members.

- **Non-Verbal Communication:** Encourage managers to express empathy non-verbally through body language, facial expressions, and tone of voice. Non-verbal cues can convey support and empathy, enhancing communication and rapport within the team.

- **Empowerment:** Empower team members with the autonomy and resources they need to succeed in their roles. Demonstrating trust and confidence in their abilities fosters a sense of ownership and accountability, motivating them to perform at their best.

- **Feedback Culture:** Cultivate a culture of feedback where constructive feedback is provided with care and empathy. Encourage managers to offer feedback sensitively, considering the feelings of team members while providing valuable insights for growth and improvement.

By implementing these practices, leaders can create a collaborative work environment where team members feel valued, supported, and empowered to collaborate effectively towards shared goals. This collaborative culture drives innovation, enhances learning, strengthens relationships, and ultimately contributes to the overall success of the organisation.

Empowerment

Empowering Leadership: Cultivating a Culture of Autonomy and Growth

Empowering employees is not just a managerial strategy; it's a philosophy that fosters a culture of trust, collaboration, and continuous growth within the organisation. Here's how leaders can empower their teams and reap the benefits of a more engaged and dynamic workforce:

1. **Encouraging Independence:** Create an environment where employees feel empowered to take the lead and drive initiatives based on their expertise and knowledge. Trust in their capabilities and encourage them to make decisions autonomously, knowing that they have been hired for a reason and are fully capable of fulfilling their responsibilities.

2. **Embracing Diverse Perspectives:** Foster an inclusive culture where opposing opinions are not only welcomed but encouraged. Recognise that diverse backgrounds and perspectives bring valuable insights and learning opportunities. Encourage open dialogue and constructive debate to enrich decision-making processes and spur innovation.

3. **Implementing Empowerment Strategies:** Empowering employees is a journey that requires deliberate strategies and ongoing effort. Provide resources, support, and

opportunities for growth to create an engaging and collaborative work environment. Empowerment strategies can include delegating authority, offering training and development programs, and fostering a culture of trust and transparency.

4. **Benefits of Empowerment:** By empowering employees, leaders can unlock numerous benefits for both individuals and the organisation. Engaged employees are more motivated, productive, and innovative. A trust-based culture reduces stress and burnout, enabling employees to take risks and learn from mistakes. This leads to better performance, a positive work environment, and increased job satisfaction.

5. **Empowerment at Multiple Levels:** Empowerment exists at various levels within the organisation. At the organisational level, it promotes a culture of collaboration and recognition. Managers play a crucial role in fostering vulnerability, clear communication, and a shared vision. Interpersonally, team members support and uplift each other, fostering a culture of mutual respect and encouragement. Individually, employees take ownership of their actions, seek out challenges, and embrace opportunities for growth.

Overall, empowering leadership is a dynamic force that not only enables self-leadership and self-reliance but also cultivates a culture of autonomy, collaboration, and continuous improvement. By empowering employees at all levels, leaders can create a workplace where individuals thrive, teams excel, and the organisation achieves its full potential.

Building a Culture of Trust: The Cornerstone of Organizational Success

In the dynamic landscape of modern organisations, cultivating a culture of trust is essential for long-term success. The trust serves as the bedrock of leadership and empowerment, fostering an environment where employees feel valued, engaged, and motivated to contribute their best. Here's how a culture of trust contributes to organisational excellence:

- **Foundation of Success:** Trust is the cornerstone of organisational success. Companies that prioritise trust experience lower employee turnover rates, heightened levels of engagement, innovation, and satisfaction. This trust extends beyond internal stakeholders to external audiences, positively impacting brand reputation and market perception.

- **Lead by Example:** Leaders play a pivotal role in establishing and nurturing trust within the organisation. Leading by example, they demonstrate transparency, inclusivity, and resilience. By empowering employees to make decisions and fostering open dialogue, leaders create an environment where trust can flourish.

- **Right People, Right Opportunities:** Hiring individuals

with the right skills, capabilities, and cultural fit is essential for building trust within teams. Assigning meaningful opportunities, providing necessary support and resources, and offering avenues for learning and growth empower employees to thrive in an autonomous environment characterised by positivity and high energy.

- **Decentralised Leadership:** Embracing decentralised leadership is key to fostering autonomy, gratitude, and accountability within the organisation. By decentralising decision-making and trusting in the expertise and commitment of managers and employees, leaders eliminate the need for micromanagement and empower teams to take ownership of their work.

- **Power vs. Influence:** Effective leaders understand the distinction between power and influence. While power may be wielded through authority, influence is earned through trust, respect, and authenticity. By leveraging influence to lead, leaders build deeper connections and foster greater trust and loyalty among their teams and followers.

In conclusion, a culture of trust is a fundamental driver of organisational excellence, enabling companies to navigate challenges, drive innovation, and achieve sustainable growth. By prioritising trust, leaders can create an environment where individuals feel empowered, valued, and inspired to contribute their best towards shared goals and aspirations.

Involving Employees in Decision-Making: Fostering Engagement and Ownership

Effective leadership goes beyond simply dictating decisions; it involves empowering employees by inviting them into the decision-making process. By involving employees in decision-making, leaders not only harness the collective intelligence of their teams but also cultivate a culture of engagement, accountability, and loyalty. Here's how involving employees in decision-making contributes to organisational success:

- **Vigilance and Due Diligence:** When employees are invited to participate in decision-making, they become more vigilant and thorough in their analysis of relevant topics or subjects. Their input adds valuable perspectives and insights, ensuring that decisions are well-informed and comprehensive.

- **Sense of Belonging and Value:** Involving employees in decision-making demonstrates that their opinions and contributions are valued and respected. This fosters a sense of belonging and ownership among employees, leading to increased motivation, engagement, and loyalty to the organisation.

- **Increased Productivity and Accountability:** Employees are often more productive when they have a say in key decisions about their work. By being actively involved in decision-making, they feel a greater sense of responsibility for the outcomes and are more committed to delivering results. Delegating tasks based on decisions made collectively enables employees to have clear responsibilities and track their progress more effectively.

- **Empowerment and Efficiency:** Empowering employees to participate in decision-making processes empowers them to take ownership of their work and contribute meaningfully to the organisation's goals. This sense of empowerment fuels efficiency and innovation, as employees are motivated to find creative solutions and drive continuous improvement.

In conclusion, involving employees in decision-making is not only a strategic leadership approach but also a catalyst for fostering a culture of engagement, ownership, and productivity within the organisation. By valuing and leveraging the insights of their teams, leaders can make more informed decisions, inspire greater commitment, and ultimately drive organisational success.

Embracing Flexible and Hybrid Work Models: Navigating the New Normal

In the wake of the 2019-2020 pandemic, the landscape of work underwent a seismic shift towards flexible hours and hybrid working schedules. This transition underscored the importance of compassion, collaboration, and adaptability, fostering an environment where employees can thrive with minimal supervision.

Offering flexible working hours and hybrid schedules presents a mutual opportunity for managers and employees to meet both performance objectives and work-life balance needs. By implementing fair policies, clear goal-setting processes, and equipping employees with the necessary tools and support for remote work, organisations can facilitate a seamless transition to flexible arrangements while retaining a sustainable workforce and promoting employee well-being.

Key considerations for organisations adopting flexible and hybrid work models include:

- **Establishing Clear Policies and Frameworks:** Developing written frameworks and principles that guide decision-making and outline expectations regarding schedules, work locations, business continuity, and reporting structures is essential. Clear policies provide employees with the necessary guidelines to navigate flexible work arrangements effectively.

- **Empowering Employees:** Empowering employees to manage their own flexibility within the established frameworks fosters a sense of autonomy and ownership. By providing employees with the flexibility to manage their schedules and work environments, organisations can promote trust, accountability, and engagement.

- **Effective Communication:** Regular and transparent communication within vertical and lateral reporting lines, as well as among coworkers, is critical. Clear communication channels ensure that employees feel supported, connected, and informed, facilitating collaboration and problem-solving in a remote or hybrid work environment.

- **Benefits for Employees and Organisations:** Flexible schedules offer numerous benefits for both employees and organisations. Employees enjoy greater control over their work hours, reduced commuting time, increased productivity, and improved work-life balance. For organisations, flexible and hybrid work arrangements can lead to higher employee satisfaction, lower office space costs, reduced absenteeism, enhanced focus, and improved retention of top talent.

As organisations navigate the transition to hybrid work, it is imperative to embrace flexibility as the new norm. By prioritising employee well-being, fostering open communication, and implementing clear policies and frameworks, organisations can effectively leverage flexible and hybrid work models to drive success in the evolving workplace landscape.

Incorporating Feedback into Organisational Culture: Fostering Open Communication and Trust

Encouraging open and honest feedback, debate, and discussions is paramount to cultivating a culture of transparency and continuous improvement within an organisation. Leaders play a pivotal role in creating an environment where employees feel empowered to voice their opinions and concerns. Here are key strategies for incorporating feedback as a central aspect of organisational culture:

- **Promote Open Communication:** Encourage a culture where open communication is valued and rewarded. Leaders should actively solicit feedback from employees and create opportunities for open dialogue, whether through regular meetings, surveys, or dedicated feedback sessions. Actively listening to employee feedback demonstrates respect and fosters a sense of trust and collaboration.

- **Participate Actively:** Leaders should actively participate in feedback sessions, demonstrating their commitment to listening and understanding employee perspectives. Engaging in meaningful discussions and addressing employee concerns proactively sends a powerful message about the importance of feedback in shaping organisational decisions and initiatives.

- **Institute an Open-Door Policy:** Implementing an open-door policy signals to employees that their voices are valued and that they have a direct line of communication with leadership. Leaders should make themselves accessible and approachable, inviting employees to share their feedback, ideas, and concerns openly. An open-door policy promotes transparency, trust, and mutual respect within the organisation.

- **Lead by Example:** Leaders should lead by example by actively seeking feedback from their teams, demonstrating receptivity to diverse viewpoints, and acting based on employee input. By modelling a culture of openness and accountability, leaders set the tone for constructive feedback exchange and empower employees to contribute to organisational success.

- **Create Visible Symbols of Openness:** Beyond verbal encouragement, leaders can create tangible symbols of openness, such as physically leaving their office doors open to signal accessibility and approachability. This visual cue reinforces the organisation's commitment to fostering a culture where feedback is welcomed and valued.

Incorporating feedback as a central component of organisational culture requires intentional effort and leadership commitment. By promoting open communication, instituting an open-door policy, leading by example, and creating visible symbols of openness, organisations can cultivate a culture of trust, collaboration, and continuous improvement where employee feedback is not only heard but also acted upon to drive positive change.

Encouraging Growth Through Trial and Error: Fostering a Culture of Learning and Empowerment

Empowering employees to take ownership of their tasks and initiatives is essential for fostering a culture of innovation and growth within an organisation. By giving people room to make mistakes and learn from them, leaders can cultivate an environment where employees feel empowered to take risks, explore new ideas, and ultimately thrive. Here's how:

- **Encourage Initiative:** Providing opportunities for employees to take charge of tasks and projects encourages them to become self-starters and proactive leaders within their respective areas. Empowering employees to take the initiative fosters a sense of ownership and accountability, driving motivation and engagement.

- **Shift from Micromanagement to Macro-Management:** Micromanagement stifles creativity and autonomy, leading to frustration and disengagement among employees. By embracing a macro-management approach, leaders provide guidance and support while giving employees the freedom to execute tasks in their own way. This shift allows employees to develop their skills and capabilities while fostering a culture of trust and empowerment.

- **Embrace Mistakes as Learning Opportunities:** Mistakes are an inevitable part of the learning process, and leaders should encourage employees to view them as opportunities for growth and development. Instead of penalising mistakes, provide constructive feedback and guidance to help employees learn from their experiences and improve their performance over time.

- **Coach and Mentor:** Adopting a coaching mindset, leaders can guide employees through challenges and help them develop problem-solving skills. Encourage open discussions where employees feel comfortable sharing their concerns and seeking guidance. By wearing the coaching hat, leaders empower employees to find their own solutions and build confidence in their abilities.

- **Promote a Culture of Continuous Learning:** Create a culture where learning is valued and supported. Provide access to training, development programs, and resources that enable employees to enhance their skills and knowledge. Encourage employees to seek out learning opportunities and continuously strive for personal and professional growth.

By giving people room to make mistakes and learn, leaders create an environment where innovation thrives and employees feel empowered to take risks and explore new ideas. This approach not only drives individual growth and development but also fosters a culture of learning, resilience, and adaptability that propels the organisation forward.

Clearing the Path to Success: Empowering Employees by Removing Obstacles

For employees to thrive and succeed in their roles, it's essential for leaders to proactively identify and remove obstacles that may impede their progress. By providing the necessary support, resources, and guidance, leaders can create an environment where employees feel empowered to excel. Here's how to remove obstacles to success:

- **Provide Necessary Tools and Resources:** Ensure that employees have access to the tools, technology, and resources they need to effectively carry out their tasks. Whether it's software, equipment, or training, investing in the right resources can streamline processes and enable employees to work more efficiently.

- **Create a Supportive Environment:** Foster a supportive work environment where employees feel comfortable seeking help and assistance when needed. Encourage open communication and collaboration among team members and be proactive in addressing any issues or concerns that arise.

- **Remove Roadblocks and Obstacles:** Identify and eliminate any barriers that may hinder progress or productivity. This could involve streamlining processes, revising policies, or reallocating resources to ensure that employees have everything they need to succeed.

- **Support Personal Challenges:** Recognise that employees may face personal challenges that impact their performance at work. Be empathetic and understanding, and offer support and flexibility as needed. Whether it's providing time off, offering counselling services, or adjusting workloads, addressing personal challenges can help employees stay focused and motivated.

- **Offer Guidance and Direction:** Set clear goals, expectations, and guidelines to help employees understand what is expected of them. Provide guidance and direction on best practices, be available to answer questions, and offer support when needed. By empowering employees with the knowledge and tools they need to succeed, leaders can help them navigate challenges and achieve their goals.

By removing obstacles to success and providing the necessary support and guidance, leaders can empower employees to perform at their best and contribute to the overall success of the organisation. This proactive approach not only enhances employee morale and engagement but also fosters a culture of accountability, collaboration, and continuous improvement.

Empowering Through Delegation and Development: Fostering Growth and Responsibility

Delegation and development are powerful tools for empowering employees and fostering their professional growth. By entrusting them with responsibilities and decision-making authority, leaders can cultivate a sense of ownership and autonomy among their team members. Here's how to effectively delegate and develop employees:

- **Empowerment Through Delegation:** Delegation involves assigning tasks, projects, or responsibilities to team members while providing them with the necessary authority and support to carry them out. Effective delegation is about more than just offloading work—it's about empowering employees to take ownership of their roles and contribute to the success of the organisation. Leaders should clearly communicate the rationale and expectations behind each delegated task, ensuring that employees understand the purpose and importance of their assignments.

- **Provide Clear Rationale and Expectations:** When delegating tasks, leaders should provide clear rationale and expectations to employees. This includes explaining why the task is important, what outcomes are expected, and how it aligns with the employee's goals and the organisation's objectives. By providing context and clarity, leaders can instil confidence in employees and empower them to approach their tasks with purpose and enthusiasm.

- **Offer Valuable Support and Guidance:** While delegating tasks, it's essential for leaders to offer ongoing support and guidance to employees. This may involve providing resources, answering questions, offering feedback, or coaching them through challenges. By offering valuable support and guidance, leaders can help employees navigate obstacles, build new skills, and grow professionally

- **Encourage Proactive Initiatives:** Empowered employees are more likely to take proactive initiatives and seek out opportunities for growth and development. Leaders should create an environment that encourages employees to explore new ideas, take risks, and challenge themselves. By fostering a culture of innovation and initiative, leaders can empower employees to drive positive change and contribute their unique talents and perspectives to the organisation.

- **Facilitate Continuous Learning and Development:** In addition to delegating tasks, leaders should actively support the ongoing learning and development of their employees. This may involve providing training opportunities, offering mentorship and coaching, or encouraging participation in professional development programs. By investing in the growth and development of their team members, leaders can empower them to reach their full potential and achieve their career goals.

By empowering employees through delegation and development, leaders can create a culture of trust, accountability, and collaboration. By entrusting them with meaningful responsibilities and providing the necessary support and guidance, leaders can foster a sense of ownership and engagement among their team members, ultimately driving success and growth for the organisation.

Facilitating Growth Opportunities: Empowering Employees to Thrive

Creating growth opportunities for employees is essential for fostering their professional development and maximising their potential. Here's how leaders can empower their team members to grow and excel:

- **Empower Employees with Autonomy:** Provide employees with opportunities to apply their knowledge, skills, and experience to complete assignments independently. Empower them with the necessary tools, resources, and authority to take ownership of their work and make decisions autonomously. By giving employees the freedom to work without constant supervision, leaders demonstrate trust and confidence in their abilities.

- **Offer Relevant Training and Development:** Invest in training and development programs that equip employees with the skills and knowledge they need to succeed. Offer workshops, courses, or mentoring opportunities that align with their career goals and professional interests. By providing relevant training and development opportunities, leaders demonstrate their commitment to supporting employees' growth and advancement.

- **Turn Challenges into Learning Opportunities:** Encourage employees to view challenges as opportunities for growth and learning. Instead of avoiding difficult tasks or projects, encourage them to embrace new challenges and step outside their comfort zone. By tackling unfamiliar or challenging assignments, employees can expand their skills, knowledge, and confidence, ultimately becoming more resilient and adaptable professionals.

- **Provide Constructive Feedback with Empathy:** Offer feedback to employees in a constructive and empathetic manner. Focus on specific behaviours or actions and provide examples of both strengths and areas for improvement. Approach feedback conversations with empathy and understanding, creating a supportive environment where employees feel valued and empowered to grow. By offering feedback that is both insightful and compassionate, leaders can help employees identify areas for growth and development while maintaining their motivation and confidence.

- **Encourage Continuous Learning and Improvement:** Foster a culture of continuous learning and improvement within the organisation. Encourage employees to seek out new opportunities for learning and skill development, whether through formal training programs, on-the-job experiences, or self-directed learning initiatives. Support their efforts to expand their knowledge and expertise and celebrate their achievements along the way. By fostering a culture of lifelong learning, leaders can empower employees to continually evolve and thrive in their careers.

By providing growth opportunities, offering relevant training and development, and fostering a culture of continuous learning, leaders can empower employees to reach their full potential and achieve their professional goals. With the right support and encouragement, employees can grow, develop, and excel, contributing to the success and growth of the organisation.

Facilitating Direct Communication: Breaking Down Bureaucratic Barriers

Removing bureaucratic constraints is crucial for fostering a culture of open communication and collaboration within an organisation. Here's how leaders can empower employees to bypass bureaucratic hurdles and engage directly with senior management:

- **Encourage Direct Communication with Leadership:** Leaders should encourage employees to communicate directly with senior management and leadership without the need for intermediaries. By eliminating unnecessary layers of hierarchy, leaders can facilitate candid, timely feedback, problem-solving, and decision-making. Employees should feel empowered to reach out to higher-ups with their ideas, concerns, or suggestions, knowing that their voices will be heard and valued.

- **Implement an Open-Door Policy:** Establishing an open-door policy creates a culture of accessibility and approachability within the organisation. Employees should feel comfortable approaching leaders at any level to discuss their thoughts, concerns, or feedback. Leaders should keep their doors figuratively and literally open, welcoming employees to engage in open and honest dialogue without fear of repercussion. This fosters trust, transparency, and collaboration across all levels of the organisation.

- **Streamline Performance Review Processes:** While performance reviews are important for evaluating employee performance and providing feedback, they should not be bogged down by bureaucratic processes. Implement a centralised performance review system that allows for direct feedback from both line managers and senior leadership. This ensures that performance evaluations are conducted fairly and transparently, with input from multiple perspectives. By involving higher leadership and human capital officials in the review process, organisations can ensure that evaluations are comprehensive and unbiased.

- **Empower Employees to Drive Change:** Leaders should empower employees to identify and address bureaucratic constraints within the organisation. Encourage employees to propose innovative solutions, streamline processes, and remove unnecessary barriers to communication and collaboration. By involving employees in the decision-making process and giving them a voice in shaping organisational policies and procedures, leaders can harness the collective intelligence and creativity of their workforce to drive meaningful change.

By removing bureaucratic constraints, implementing an open-door policy, streamlining performance review processes, and empowering employees to drive change, leaders can create a more agile, responsive, and inclusive organisation. By fostering a culture of direct communication and collaboration, organisations can break down barriers, unlock creativity, and drive innovation and growth.

Employee Recognition: Fostering Growth and Appreciation

Recognising employees for their hard work goes beyond simple acknowledgement—it involves creating opportunities for holistic self-improvement and growth. Here's how leaders can effectively recognise and appreciate employees while fostering their development:

- **Offer Opportunities for Holistic Self-Improvement:** Encourage employees to continuously enhance their skills and knowledge, both professionally and personally. Provide access to training programs, workshops, and resources that enable employees to learn new skills and develop their talents. Support initiatives that promote work-life balance and well-being, such as flexible scheduling, wellness programs, or personal development courses. By investing in employees' growth and development, leaders demonstrate their commitment to their team members' long-term success and fulfillment .

- **Motivate Continuous Learning and Growth:** Inspire employees to pursue growth opportunities and strive for excellence in all aspects of their lives. Encourage them to set ambitious goals, take on new challenges, and expand their horizons. Foster a culture of curiosity, innovation, and continuous improvement where employees feel empowered to explore new ideas and approaches. By promoting a growth mindset and celebrating achievements, leaders motivate employees to reach their full potential and contribute their best to the organisation's success.

- **Forgive Mistakes and Encourage Risk-Taking: Create** a supportive environment where employees feel comfortable taking risks and making mistakes. Emphasise the importance of learning from failures and setbacks as valuable opportunities for growth and development. Encourage employees to step outside their comfort zones, experiment with new ideas, and push the boundaries of their capabilities. By forgiving mistakes and encouraging resilience, leaders build trust and confidence within their teams and foster a culture of innovation and creativity.

- **Show Appreciation and Acknowledge Contributions:** Regularly recognise and appreciate employees for their hard work, dedication, and contributions to the team's success. Take the time to acknowledge individual achievements, milestones, and efforts that go above and beyond expectations. Celebrate team accomplishments and milestones collectively to foster a sense of camaraderie and shared success. Genuine appreciation and recognition not only boost morale and motivation but also reinforce positive behaviours and performance.

By offering opportunities for holistic self-improvement, motivating continuous learning and growth, forgiving mistakes, and showing genuine appreciation for contributions, leaders can create a culture of recognition and appreciation that inspires employees to excel and thrive. This fosters a positive work environment where employees feel valued, empowered, and motivated to achieve their personal and professional goals.

04

Simplifying

strategy

"

Simplifying strategy

Embrace simplicity; it's the master key to brilliance.

- PREEA V MANE

KEEP IT SIMPLE

Simplifying strategy is key to its effectiveness. A strategy should be clear, straightforward, and intuitive, based on market realities and identified trends. It doesn't need to be complex or convoluted; rather, it should be easily comprehensible and communicable across all levels of the organisation. A truly great strategy doesn't require an army of consultants or complicated spreadsheets to explain; it can be succinctly summarised and readily understood by everyone.

Many companies invest significant resources in crafting elaborate strategies, only to find them falling short of expectations. This can lead to frustration and a sense of wasted effort. As former General Electric CEO Jack Welch noted, "In real life, strategy is actually very straightforward. You pick a general direction and implement it like hell."

The essence of a successful strategy lies in its simplicity, clarity, and adaptability. Keeping it simple ensures that leaders can effectively communicate and implement it throughout the organisation. This simplicity provides a clear path forward for all stakeholders, facilitating effective resource allocation and minimising the risk of miscommunication or misalignment.

As exemplified by Steve Jobs, simplicity may be challenging to achieve, but it is ultimately more powerful than complexity. Jobs famously said, "Simple. Harder than complex. But with it, you can move mountains." This ethos underscores the importance of simplicity in strategy, as it enables organisations to navigate complexities with clarity and purpose.

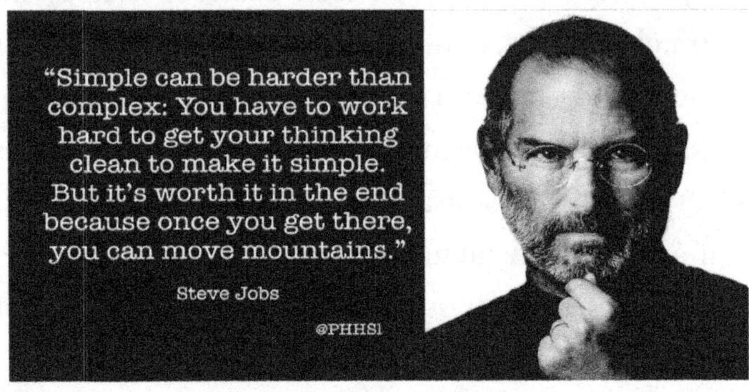

The success story of Apple under Steve Jobs provides a compelling illustration of the power of simplicity in strategy. In 1997, when Jobs returned to Apple, he inherited a complex and convoluted product lineup that included numerous computer models, peripherals, and accessories. Recognising the unsustainable nature of this approach, Jobs embarked on a mission to simplify Apple's product portfolio.

Jobs streamlined the lineup to a simple 2x2 matrix consisting of four product categories: desktops and portables for consumers and desktops and portables for professionals. This bold move allowed Apple to focus its resources and efforts on producing a limited set of products that were not only easy to understand but also distinctly differentiated from competitors. This strategic pivot played a pivotal role in Apple's eventual resurgence and transformation into one of the most valuable companies in the world.

The case of Apple underscores the importance of simplicity in strategy, particularly in today's fast-paced and dynamic business environment. However, it's essential to clarify the distinction between a simple strategy and a simplistic one.

A simple strategy is clear, concise, and easy to understand, yet it doesn't oversimplify or ignore the complexities of the situation. It involves thorough analysis, considering all relevant factors, options, and potential scenarios. Moreover, executing a simple strategy requires dedication and relentless effort in both planning and implementation.

As Albert Einstein famously said, "Make everything as simple as possible, but not simpler." This quote encapsulates the essence of simplicity in strategy — it should strive for clarity and efficiency without sacrificing depth or effectiveness. Oversimplification can lead to overlooking critical factors and failing to address the complexity of the situation, ultimately undermining the strategy's success.

Conversely, a simplistic strategy is overly simplistic, lacking depth and failing to acknowledge the intricacies of the problem. It tends to trivialise the issue and sidestep the core challenges rather than confronting them directly. Consequently, a simplistic strategy is ineffective because it fails to provide meaningful solutions to complex problems.

In conclusion, while simplicity in strategy is desirable, it's crucial to strike the right balance between simplicity and depth. A simple strategy that acknowledges and addresses the complexities of the situation is far more likely to succeed than one that oversimplifies or ignores critical factors.

Simplicity in strategy is indeed valuable, but it's essential to strike a balance between simplicity and a thorough understanding of the complexities at play. While simplicity can enhance clarity and effectiveness, oversimplification can be detrimental to the strategy's success.

An oversimplified, or simplistic, strategy fails to adequately address the nuances and intricacies of the problem at hand. Instead of targeting the core of the issue, it often trivialises or sidesteps the underlying complexities, leading to ineffective solutions. Therefore, a simplistic strategy is inherently flawed and unlikely to achieve meaningful results.

The distinction between a simple and simplistic strategy is crucial. A simple strategy is clear, concise, and easy to understand, yet it doesn't ignore or oversimplify the complexities of the situation. It involves thorough analysis and consideration of all relevant factors, options, and potential scenarios. A simple strategy strikes the right balance between clarity and depth, providing a clear path forward while acknowledging the intricacies of the problem.

Creating a simple strategy is no easy feat. It requires careful thought, analysis, and decision-making to distil complex concepts or strategies into straightforward, actionable plans. While it may be tempting to opt for elaborate, detailed strategies, simplicity often prevails, particularly in today's fast-paced, information-saturated world.

Simplification facilitates comprehension, absorption, and action, making it easier for stakeholders to grasp and implement the strategy effectively. By articulating issues plainly and using accessible language, leaders can swiftly convey key points and rally support for the strategy. In an era marked by noise, distractions, and shrinking attention spans, communication clarity is paramount, and simplicity in strategy ensures that key messages resonate with stakeholders.

Ultimately, while complexity may abound, focusing on simplicity and fundamental aspects remains the most effective strategy for navigating today's challenges. By embracing simplicity in strategy development and communication, organisations can cut through the noise, foster understanding, and drive meaningful action toward achieving their goals.

In today's bustling and intricate business environment, making a lasting impression doesn't require bombast or excessive complexity. Instead, it hinges on presenting a composed and thoughtful demeanour while offering easily digestible value propositions. Articulating what you bring to the table, why it matters to customers, and how it enhances their lives, whether by saving time, boosting profits, or honing skills, is paramount.

In our interactions with various organisations, we often encounter intelligent and well-intentioned individuals. However, it's surprising how many tend to complicate their communication unnecessarily.

To clarify, there's a distinction between simplicity and oversimplification. Simplifying a complex idea involves distilling it down to its essence without misrepresenting or omitting crucial elements. Oversimplification, on the other hand, entails stripping away too much complexity, resulting in a shallow understanding of the subject and overlooking important aspects.

The "Keep it Simple and Straightforward" (KISS) principle encapsulates this approach succinctly. It advocates for brevity and clarity in communication, urging individuals to convey their message in a concise and understandable manner. This principle finds resonance in diverse fields, including design and military strategy.

A prime example of the KISS principle in action can be observed in Apple's product design philosophy. Apple prioritises simplicity and user-friendly interfaces, enabling users of all skill levels to navigate their products effortlessly. By eliminating unnecessary elements and focusing on functionality and intuitive design, Apple exemplifies the KISS principle, making their products accessible and appealing to a broad audience.

In military strategy, the KISS approach emphasises crafting plans and systems characterised by simplicity and clarity. Clear and executable plans are essential for preventing misunderstandings and errors and facilitating the efficient achievement of objectives.

When it comes to strategy crafting, simplicity often reigns supreme. Exceptional strategies are often disarmingly simple yet profoundly effective. While formulating a strategy may seem daunting, remember that the most successful ideas are often the simplest and most obvious ones.

Ultimately, the KISS principle underscores the importance of clarity and accessibility in communication and design. By embracing simplicity and avoiding unnecessary complexity, organisations can enhance user experiences, streamline operations, and achieve greater success in today's competitive landscape.

Unveiling the Obvious: The Essence of Outstanding Strategies

Outstanding strategies often possess a quality of being glaringly obvious. When we look back at successful strategies, they often seem like common sense in hindsight. This is because they are exceptionally well-aligned with the organisation's needs and the demands of the market.

In essence, these exceptional strategies are hiding in plain sight. The challenge lies in recognising them and summoning the courage to pursue them. While it can be difficult to see the forest for the trees, taking a step back to examine the broader picture can unveil the most apparent yet potent strategies.

Once an exceptional strategy emerges, it may seem as though it has always existed, awaiting discovery. Looking back, it may be perplexing to contemplate how such an evident solution could have been overlooked. However, the process of formulating an outstanding strategy is far from straightforward. It demands a profound comprehension of the circumstances, the capacity to view matters from various angles, and the ingenuity to devise a distinctive and efficacious solution.

Should you encounter challenges in crafting an 'obvious' strategy, several practical steps can be taken. It's imperative to approach the issue from diverse perspectives and challenge any assumptions that might constrain your thinking. Employing techniques of repeatedly asking "why" to delve into the root cause of a problem. When you distil your strategic gaps to their essence, the appropriate course of action often becomes apparent. Additionally, seeking out varied viewpoints and insights from customers, employees, or industry experts can be invaluable. Furthermore, staying abreast of industry trends and continually analysing data can help pinpoint potential areas for enhancement. By amalgamating these approaches, you can begin to unveil the "obvious" strategies that may have been concealed in plain sight.

The Art of Strategy Sharing: Inspiring Innovation Through Emulation

Exceptional strategies serve as beacons of innovation and success in the business world, guiding organisations towards achieving their goals and staying ahead of the competition. While the term "imitation" may carry connotations of copying or lack of originality, in the realm of strategy, it embodies a powerful principle: the recognition and replication of effective tactics and approaches.

Successful organisations understand that reinventing the wheel is not always necessary. Instead, they actively seek out and study the strategies of their peers, competitors, and even unrelated industries. This process of strategic borrowing and adaptation allows them to capitalise on existing knowledge and proven methodologies, saving time and resources while increasing the likelihood of success.

However, strategic emulation does not mean blindly copying what others are doing. Rather, it involves a careful analysis of the underlying principles and mechanisms behind successful strategies. By understanding the rationale and context behind these strategies, organisations can tailor them to their own unique circumstances and objectives.

Furthermore, the process of seeking inspiration from others extends beyond traditional channels. Industry publications, conferences, networking events, and even informal conversations with industry peers can all provide valuable insights and perspectives. By maintaining an open mind and a willingness to learn from others, organisations can continuously refine and evolve their strategic approaches.

Moreover, exceptional strategies are not meant to be hoarded as proprietary secrets. Instead, they are intended to be shared and replicated. When a strategy proves to be truly remarkable, it often gains traction not only within the organisation that developed it but also among competitors and industry peers. This widespread adoption serves as a testament to the strategy's effectiveness and universal applicability.

In essence, the emulation of exceptional strategies represents a symbiotic relationship within the business ecosystem. By sharing and adopting successful tactics, organisations collectively raise the bar for innovation and excellence, driving progress and success across industries. Therefore, embracing strategic imitation as a proactive and collaborative approach can lead to sustained growth and competitive advantage in today's dynamic business landscape.

The Power of Simplicity: Maximising Impact and Creating Value

Keeping things simple is often touted as a guiding principle in various aspects of life, including business, design, communication, and problem-solving. But why exactly is simplicity so highly valued? The answer lies in its ability to maximise impact and create significant value.

- **Clarity and Focus:** Simple solutions cut through complexity and noise, providing clarity and focus on what truly matters. By stripping away unnecessary elements, you can direct attention to the core essence of a problem or idea. This clarity enables better decision-making and empowers individuals and teams to take decisive action.

- **Accessibility:** Complexity can be alienating, while simplicity is inclusive. Simple solutions are easier to understand and navigate, making them accessible to a broader audience. Whether you're communicating with colleagues, customers, or stakeholders, simplicity ensures that your message resonates and is understood by everyone.

- **Efficiency and Effectiveness:** Simplicity streamlines processes, reducing friction and inefficiencies. When tasks are straightforward and uncomplicated, they can be completed more efficiently, saving time and resources. Simple systems are also more resilient and adaptable, capable of responding quickly to changing circumstances.

- **Memorability:** Simple ideas are more memorable and impactful. They stick in people's minds, driving engagement and action. Whether it's a catchy slogan, a user-friendly product interface, or a straightforward business strategy, simplicity enhances memorability and leaves a lasting impression.

- **Innovation and Creativity:** Simplifying complex concepts or problems often requires innovative thinking. By distilling ideas down to their core components, you're forced to find novel approaches and creative solutions. Simplicity fosters innovation by encouraging out-of-the-box thinking and challenging conventional wisdom.

- **Customer Satisfaction:** In today's fast-paced world, customers crave simplicity and convenience. Products and services that are easy to use and understand are more likely to win customer loyalty and satisfaction. By prioritising simplicity in design and user experience, businesses can enhance customer satisfaction and build strong relationships.

- **Resilience and Adaptability:** Simple solutions are inherently more agile and adaptable. They can be scaled up or down, modified, and repurposed to meet evolving needs and challenges. In a constantly changing environment, simplicity provides a solid foundation for resilience and long-term success.

In summary, simplicity is not about compromising quality or depth; rather, it's about distilling complexity into its most essential elements. By embracing simplicity, you can amplify your impact, create meaningful value, and navigate complexity with clarity and confidence. Simplifying complexity goes beyond just making things easier to understand; it's about unlocking the full potential of your ideas and endeavours. Here's a deeper dive into why simplicity is crucial for maximising impact and creating substantial value:

- **Clarity and Focus:** Complexity often clouds understanding and dilutes the impact of your message or strategy. By simplifying complex concepts or processes, you bring clarity and focus to the forefront. This clarity enables stakeholders to grasp the essence of your message swiftly and decisively, aligning their actions with your objectives.

- **Efficiency and Effectiveness:** Simple solutions are inherently more efficient and effective. By streamlining workflows, reducing redundancy, and eliminating unnecessary steps, you optimise resource allocation and accelerate progress towards your goals. This efficiency translates into tangible results, enabling you to achieve objectives more swiftly and with greater impact.

- **Accessibility:** Complexity can be a barrier to engagement and adoption. In contrast, simplicity makes information and solutions accessible to a broader audience. Whether it's customers, employees, or partners, simplicity ensures that everyone can engage with your ideas and offerings, thereby maximising their impact and value.

- **User Experience:** In today's fast-paced world, user experience is paramount. Complex interfaces or processes can frustrate users and deter engagement. By prioritising simplicity in product design or service delivery, you enhance the user experience, fostering loyalty and satisfaction. This positive user experience translates into increased adoption, retention, and advocacy.

- **Innovation:** Simple solutions often pave the way for innovation. By challenging conventional wisdom and embracing simplicity, you encourage creative thinking and novel approaches. This openness to simplicity can lead to breakthroughs that revolutionise industries and create significant value, driving growth and competitive advantage.

Ultimately, simplicity is about distilling complexity into its most potent and impactful form. It's not about sacrificing depth or sophistication but rather about unlocking the true potential of your ideas and endeavours. By keeping it simple, you empower yourself to make a greater impact, create more value, and drive meaningful change in the world.

Unveiling the Power of Simplicity: Understanding its Key Attributes

Simplicity possesses an inherent power that stems from its ability to enhance various aspects of communication, problem-solving, and innovation. Here's a closer look at why simplicity is such a potent force:

- **Clarity:** Simplifying complex ideas or processes distils them to their essence, making them easier to understand and convey. This clarity reduces confusion, ambiguity, and misinterpretation, fostering more effective communication and decision-making.

- **Memorability:** Simple concepts are more memorable because they are easier to grasp and retain. By presenting information in a straightforward manner, you enhance learning and facilitate quicker recall, enabling individuals to access and apply knowledge more efficiently.

- **Accessibility:** Simplicity ensures that information and solutions are accessible to a wider audience. Complex ideas can be intimidating or exclusive, but simplicity makes content inclusive and understandable to people from diverse backgrounds and skill levels.

- **Efficiency:** Simple solutions tend to be more efficient as they eliminate unnecessary complexity and streamline processes. By reducing friction and resource requirements, simplicity enables faster decision-making, smoother execution, and optimal resource allocation.

- **Innovation:** Embracing simplicity can spur innovation by encouraging creative thinking and novel approaches. Challenging conventional wisdom and seeking elegant solutions often leads to breakthroughs that revolutionise industries and drive progress.

- **User Experience:** In today's digital age, simplicity is highly valued in user experience design. Products and services that are intuitive, user-friendly, and devoid of unnecessary complexity tend to attract and retain users, enhancing satisfaction, loyalty, and engagement.

By harnessing the power of simplicity, individuals and organisations can unlock new opportunities, drive meaningful change, and create solutions that resonate with a broader audience. Whether in communication, problem-solving, or product design, simplicity remains a cornerstone of effective and impactful solutions.

The Role of Simplicity in the Path to Success: Understanding its Impact

While simplicity is indeed a powerful tool in the journey toward success, it's important to recognise that success is multifaceted and influenced by a myriad of factors. Nonetheless, simplicity often plays a pivotal role in several critical aspects of success:

- **Communication:** Clear and straightforward communication is indispensable for effective collaboration and alignment. Simplicity ensures that messages are easily understood and embraced by team members, stakeholders, and customers alike, fostering cohesion and driving progress.

- **Problem-Solving:** Simplifying complex problems facilitates more efficient and effective solutions. By breaking down challenges into manageable components and removing unnecessary layers of complexity, individuals and organisations can devise actionable strategies to overcome obstacles and achieve their objectives.

- **User Experience:** In today's consumer-centric landscape, simplicity is paramount for a positive user experience. Products and services that are intuitive, user-friendly, and devoid of unnecessary complexity resonate more with consumers, fostering loyalty, satisfaction, and, ultimately, success.

- **Execution:** Streamlining processes and workflows through simplicity enhances efficiency and facilitates seamless execution. By eliminating unnecessary steps and optimising resource allocation, individuals and organisations can achieve their goals more effectively and expediently.

- **Adaptability:** Simple solutions are inherently more adaptable and resilient in the face of change. Complexity can hinder agility and flexibility, making it challenging to respond swiftly to evolving circumstances. Simplicity enables organisations to pivot more easily and navigate through uncertainty with greater ease.

- **Scalability:** Simple systems and strategies are easier to scale and replicate across different contexts or markets. Scalability is crucial for sustainable growth and expansion, as it allows organisations to maintain consistency and coherence while accommodating increased demand or diversification.

While simplicity undoubtedly contributes significantly to success, it's essential to strike a balance and acknowledge that complexity may be warranted in certain situations. Success often requires a nuanced approach that considers various factors, including the specific context, goals, and challenges at hand. Therefore, while simplicity serves as an asset, it is just one piece of the puzzle in the pursuit of success.

Mastering Simplicity: Practical Tips for Streamlining Work Processes

Simplicity is not just a desirable quality in the workplace; it's a powerful approach that can enhance productivity, clarity, and effectiveness. Here are some practical tips on how to keep things simple at work:

- **Clarify Goals and Priorities:** Begin by clearly defining your goals and priorities. Identify the most critical tasks and focus your energy on accomplishing them. Avoid spreading yourself too thin by taking on unnecessary objectives that could dilute your efforts.

- **Streamline Processes:** Evaluate existing workflows and look for opportunities to streamline processes. Identify bottlenecks, redundancies, or inefficiencies, and seek ways to simplify or automate tasks. Streamlining processes saves time and resources, leading to increased productivity and smoother operations.

- **Communicate Clearly:** Effective communication is essential for simplicity in the workplace. Use clear and concise language when communicating with colleagues, clients, or stakeholders. Avoid using jargon or overly technical terms that could confuse or alienate others. Transparency and straightforwardness foster mutual understanding.

- **Focus on Essential Information:** When presenting information or data, focus on the key points. Avoid overwhelming your audience with excessive details or irrelevant information. Highlight insights that are relevant to the discussion or decision-making process, keeping the focus on what truly matters.

- **Set Clear Expectations:** Establish clear expectations for yourself and your team members. Define roles, responsibilities, and deadlines to avoid confusion or misunderstandings. Provide clear guidance to ensure everyone knows what is expected of them, fostering accountability and clarity.

- **Simplify Meetings:** Keep meetings focused and productive by setting clear agendas and objectives in advance. Stick to the agenda and discourage tangents or unnecessary discussions. Encourage active participation and collaboration while minimising time wasted on irrelevant topics.

- **Embrace Minimalism:** Adopt a minimalist approach to work and decision-making. Focus on doing fewer things but doing them well. Avoid unnecessary complexity or over-engineering solutions. Strive for simplicity in design, processes, and problem-solving, aiming for elegant and effective solutions.

- **Seek Feedback and Iterate:** Continuously seek feedback from colleagues, clients, or customers to identify areas for improvement. Use feedback to iterate and refine your processes, products, or services. Keep an open mind and be willing to adapt and evolve as needed, embracing a culture of continuous improvement.

By embracing these strategies and cultivating a mindset of simplicity, you can streamline work processes, improve communication, and increase overall efficiency and effectiveness in the workplace.

The Power of Simplicity: Unlocking Benefits in Life and Work

Simplicity isn't just a preference; it's a powerful approach that yields numerous benefits across various aspects of life and work. Let's delve into the advantages of keeping things simple:

- **Clarity:** Simplification brings clarity. Clear communication and understanding lead to fewer misunderstandings, better decision-making, and, ultimately, better outcomes. By distilling complex ideas or processes into their essential components, you can enhance clarity and effectiveness in your endeavours.

- **Efficiency:** Simple solutions are inherently more efficient. By removing unnecessary steps or complexities, you can streamline workflows, save time, and optimise resource utilisation. This efficiency translates into increased productivity and smoother operations.

- **Focus:** Simplification helps you focus on what truly matters. By eliminating distractions or non-essential tasks, you can direct your energy and attention towards high-priority goals and objectives, enhancing your ability to achieve meaningful results.

- **Accessibility:** Simple solutions are more accessible to a wider audience. Whether you're communicating ideas, designing products, or delivering services, simplicity ensures that everyone can engage and benefit, regardless of their background or expertise. This inclusivity fosters greater engagement and satisfaction among stakeholders.

- **User Experience:** In product design and service delivery, simplicity is paramount for a positive user experience. Intuitive, easy-to-use products and services resonate more with consumers, fostering loyalty and satisfaction. By prioritising simplicity, you can enhance user engagement and drive business success.

- **Innovation:** Embracing simplicity can stimulate innovation. By challenging conventional wisdom and seeking elegant, uncomplicated solutions, you encourage creative thinking and novel approaches. This innovative mindset can lead to breakthroughs that revolutionise industries and drive progress.

- **Reduced Stress:** Simplifying your life or work can reduce stress and overwhelm. By decluttering your environment, organising tasks, and setting clear priorities, you create a sense of calm and control, leading to improved well-being and productivity.

- **Cost Savings:** Simplification can lead to cost savings. By eliminating inefficiencies, reducing waste, and improving productivity, you can lower operational costs and increase profitability. Simplifying processes or systems can also lead to more efficient resource allocation, further enhancing cost-effectiveness.

- **Scalability:** Simple systems or strategies are easier to scale and replicate across different contexts or markets. Scalability is essential for sustainable growth and expansion, enabling organisations to maintain consistency and coherence while accommodating increased demand or diversification.

In summary, embracing simplicity offers a wide array of benefits, from improved clarity and efficiency to enhanced user experience and innovation. By prioritising simplicity in your approach to life and work, you can unlock these benefits and achieve greater success and satisfaction.

The Multifaceted Virtues of Simplicity

"Simplicity" is not merely the absence of complexity; it encapsulates a spectrum of virtues that enhance various aspects of life and work. Let's explore what lies within simplicity:

- **Clarity:** Simplicity brings clarity by removing unnecessary layers and complications. This clarity fosters better understanding, communication, and decision-making, allowing the essence of ideas or concepts to shine through with precision.

- **Efficiency:** Simplification enhances efficiency by streamlining processes and eliminating redundancies. By optimising resource utilisation and minimising waste, simplicity ensures tasks are completed promptly and with minimal effort.

- **Focus:** Simplicity helps maintain focus on essential tasks or goals by eliminating distractions. With a clear vision and streamlined approach, individuals can direct their energy towards high-impact activities, accelerating progress and achieving objectives more effectively.

- **Accessibility:** Simple solutions are accessible to a broader audience, regardless of background or expertise. By removing unnecessary complexities, simplicity ensures that everyone can engage and benefit, fostering inclusivity and widening the reach of offerings.

- **Innovation:** Embracing simplicity stimulates innovation by encouraging creative thinking and novel approaches. By challenging conventional wisdom and seeking elegant solutions, simplicity fosters breakthroughs and advancements in various domains.

- **Elegance:** Simplicity is synonymous with elegance, characterised by effectiveness and aesthetic appeal. Elegant solutions are intuitive, refined, and easy to use or understand, enhancing user experience and perception of quality.

- **Resilience:** Simple systems or strategies are often more resilient in the face of change. By reducing fragility and vulnerability introduced by complexity, simplicity fosters agility and flexibility, enabling quicker responses to challenges or disruptions.

- **Peace of Mind:** Simplifying life or work brings peace of mind by creating a sense of calm and control. Decluttering environments, organising tasks, and setting clear priorities reduce stress, enhance well-being, and promote overall satisfaction.

In essence, simplicity embodies virtues such as clarity, efficiency, focus, accessibility, innovation, elegance, resilience, and peace of mind. By embracing simplicity in both work and life, individuals unlock these virtues, paving the way for greater success, fulfilment, and overall well-being.

The Power of Simplicity in Business

Simplicity is not just a preference but a necessity in the dynamic landscape of business. Here's why simplicity holds such importance:

- **Clarity and Communication:** In the noisy marketplace, clear messaging is crucial. Simple, concise communication ensures that company goals, product features, and marketing messages are easily understood by both internal teams and external stakeholders.

- **User Experience:** Customer satisfaction hinges on the ease of interaction with products and services. Simple, intuitive designs enhance usability and foster customer loyalty by minimising confusion and frustration.

- **Efficiency and Productivity:** Complex workflows can bog down productivity. Simplified operations streamline tasks, reduce friction, and empower employees to work more effectively, accomplishing more in less time.

- **Decision-Making:** Informed decisions rely on clear, concise information. Simplified data and analysis enable executives and managers to grasp key insights quickly, leading to better strategic decisions that drive business success.

- **Innovation:** Simplification sparks creativity. By challenging the status quo and seeking elegant solutions, businesses uncover new opportunities for improvement and differentiation, driving innovation and staying ahead of the curve.

- **Scalability:** Simple business models are easier to scale. Complexity can impede growth by introducing barriers and inefficiencies. Simplifying operations and strategies enables businesses to expand more efficiently and sustainably.

- **Cost Reduction:** Complexity often comes with a price tag. Simplifying processes and operations can lead to cost savings by reducing overhead, streamlining resource allocation, and optimising efficiencies.

- **Competitive Advantage:** In a crowded marketplace, simplicity can be a powerful differentiator. Businesses that offer simple, intuitive solutions stand out from the competition and attract customers seeking ease of use and convenience.

In essence, simplicity drives clarity, efficiency, innovation, and competitiveness in business. By embracing simplicity in all aspects of operations, businesses can streamline processes, enhance communication, and deliver exceptional experiences that set them apart in today's fast-paced environment.

Deciphering Complexity: Understanding the Difference Between Easy and Simple

"Easy" and "simple" are often used interchangeably, but they convey distinct meanings, each essential in understanding tasks and concepts:

- **Easy:** "Easy" refers to the level of difficulty or effort required to accomplish a task or understand a concept. It denotes a sense of minimal exertion, skill, or complication associated with completing a task. What makes a task easy can vary significantly based on individual capabilities, experience, or circumstances. For one person, a task might be effortless, requiring little time or expertise, while for another, it could pose significant challenges. For instance, solving a basic math problem might be easy for someone with a strong math background but challenging for someone with limited mathematical skills.

- **Simple:** "Simple," in contrast, pertains to the degree of complexity or intricacy of something. It implies that something is uncomplicated, straightforward, or easy to understand. Simplicity often entails clarity, efficiency, and elegance in design or execution. A simple solution involves minimal steps, components, or features, yet it effectively achieves its intended purpose. For example, a streamlined user interface on a website or a straightforward recipe with few ingredients demonstrates simplicity. Simple solutions prioritise essential elements while minimising unnecessary complexities.

In essence, while "easy" relates to the effort or difficulty level required to complete a task, "simple" pertains to the complexity or intricacy of the task itself. It's essential to distinguish between the two because a task may be easy but not necessarily simple, or vice versa. For instance, solving a complex mathematical problem may require significant effort and skill, yet the solution itself could be simple and elegant. Conversely, a task may be straightforward and uncomplicated, making it simple, but it might still require effort or skill to accomplish, making it not necessarily easy. Understanding this distinction helps individuals navigate tasks and concepts more effectively, appreciating both the effort involved and the underlying simplicity or complexity inherent in them.

Closing Words

As we come to the end of this journey through the realms of strategy, leadership, and management, I am filled with gratitude for the opportunity to share insights, experiences, and reflections with you, the reader. Whether you've been a seasoned professional seeking new perspectives or a curious enthusiast eager to learn, I hope this book has provided valuable insights and practical strategies to inspire your journey.

In crafting this book, I have drawn upon a wealth of knowledge gained through education, research, training, and hands-on experience in various organisational settings. However, I recognise that no single book can encompass the entirety of this vast and dynamic field. Therefore, while I have endeavoured to cover a wide range of topics, I acknowledge that there may be areas left unexplored or perspectives not fully represented.

I invite you to approach this book with an open mind and a willingness to engage with its contents. Whether the insights resonate deeply with you or challenge your existing beliefs, I encourage you to reflect on how they may apply to your own context and experiences.

Should you have any comments, questions, or feedback, I welcome you to reach out to me directly at author@preeavmane.com . Your insights are invaluable and will help inform future editions of this book, ensuring that it continues to evolve and meet the needs of readers like you.

In closing, I extend my heartfelt thanks to you for accompanying me on this journey. May the knowledge and wisdom shared within these pages empower you to lead with purpose, navigate with clarity, and manage with excellence in all your endeavours.

Warmest regards,

PREEA V MANE

Additional Resources

REFERENCES:

Michael E. Porter HBR's 10 must reads What is strategy.

Tom Rath Barry Conchie StrengthsFinder

The Power of Strategic Workforce Planning - i-l-m.com

https://www.n2growth.com/leadership-and-perception/

https://economictimes.indiatimes.com/jobs/c-suite/the-impact-of-leadership-on-organizational-culture-and-employee-morale/articleshow/104629435.cms?from=mdr

https://www.businessnewsdaily.com/7481-leadership-quotes.html

Wagner & Hollenbeck Organisational behaviour securing competitive advantage.

Leadership Lessons from Bhagavad Gita1 B Mahadevan2

https://en.wikipedia.org/wiki/Influence_of_Bhagavad_Gita

https://timesofindia.indiatimes.com/readersblog/bhagavadgita/the-bhagavad-gitas-impact-on-life-and-leadership-44934/

https://www.gallup.com/workplace/231593/why-great-managers-rare.aspx

https://www.forbes.com/sites/theyec/2023/06/21/empathetic-leadership-in-the-digital-age-nurturing-innovation-and-resilience-in-the-workplace/?sh=6b8c7796146e

https://hbr.org/2021/09/the-future-of-flexibility-at-work

https://cpdonline.co.uk/knowledge-base/safeguarding/types-of-bias/

https://committees.parliament.uk/writtenevidence/22776/html/

https://www.masterclass.com/articles/how-to-identify-bias

https://lesroches.edu/blog/what-different-management-styles/

https://online.hbs.edu/blog/post/leadership-vs-management

https://hbr.org/1996/11/what-is-strategy

https://www.indeed.com/career-advice/career-development/strengths-and-weaknesses-of-management

https://high5test.com/leadership-strengths/

https://online.hbs.edu/blog/post/what-is-business-strategy

https://in.indeed.com/career-advice/career-development/business-strategy

https://www.thestrategyinstitute.org/insights/what-is-business-strategy-definition-importance-levels-and-examples

https://consulterce.com/business-strategy/#strategy-success

https://www.marvilano.com/post/why-strategy-must-be-simple

https://www.cssp.com/can-a-strategic-plan-be-too-simple/

Made in the USA
Monee, IL
07 July 2026

56550115R00163